HOMŒOPATHY

AND

ALLOPATHY.

Homœopathy and Allopathy:

REPLY

TO

"AN EXAMINATION OF THE DOCTRINES AND EVIDENCES OF

HOMŒOPATHY,

BY WORTHINGTON HOOKER, M. D."

By E. E. MARCY, M. D.,

AUTHOR OF "THE HOMŒOPATHIC THEORY AND PRACTICE OF MEDICINE."

"Nor stands a fact
Less in repute, because an empty jest
Has cracked thereon, and shown its hollowness."
BOKER.

"No cheek is known to blush, or heart to throb,
Save when they lose a question or a job."
POPE.

NEW-YORK:
WILLIAM RADDE, 322 BROADWAY.
C. L. RADEMACHER & SHEEK, 239 ARCH-STREET, PHILADELPHIA;
OTIS CLAPP, SCHOOL-STREET, BOSTON;
J. G. WESSELHŒFT, 64 FOURTH STREET, ST. LOUIS.

1852.

Angell, Engel & Hewitt, Printers, 1 Spruce-st.

TO

WILLIAM CULLEN BRYANT

THE MOST ILLUSTRIOUS OF

THE LIVING AUTHORS OF AMERICA,

WHO HAS GIVEN THE

POWERFUL SUPPORT OF HIS GENIUS TO THE GREAT LAW OF

"SIMILIA SIMILIBUS CURANTUR,"

THIS REFUTATION OF A SUPERFICIAL AND MENDACIOUS ATTACK UPON THAT LAW,

Is Respectfully Inscribed,

BY HIS ADMIRER AND OBEDIENT SERVANT,

E. E. MARCY.

PREFACE.

THE extraordinary advances made by the homœopathic principles of medicine, have induced in the last two years an opposition unprecedented for activity, earnestness, and virulence. On their first promulgation in America, while they had the character of novelty, and few except disciples had any definite acquaintance with them, two or three of the leading physicians of the allopathic school attacked them in pamphlets, in one case at least remarkable for a ready wit and most felicitous manner. It will be understood that we refer to Dr. Holmes. Since the publication of his trifling, superficial, but brilliant essay, the master minds of the Old School, probably from a more familiar acquaintance with the subject, and a conviction that "discretion," in this case, was "the best part of valor," have generally been silent, and the attacks upon the Philosophical Method of Cure have been confined to the meaner and least scrupulous allopathic physicians, the class which in all professions, occupations, and conditions, is content for a small reward and a little notoriety to do the baser work for which there is supposed to be an occasion or a necessity.

For a certain insolence of tone, rather than for any peculiar talent or freshness exhibited in it, a volume entitled "Homœopathy: an Examination of its Doctrines and Evidences, by Worthington Hooker, M. D.," has recently attracted some notice. It contains, indeed, nothing of fact, conclusion, or suggestion, that had not been said often before, and in a more pungent and attractive manner, but—possibly for the fortunate selection of a publisher—the book has had some currency, and in the following pages we have taken the trouble to answer it; not that it deserved for its own qualities any such attention, but that in one exposure this whole class of feeble, false, and malicious attacks upon Homœopathy might be refuted.

The progress of Homœopathy is an apparent and altogether unquestionable fact in the recent history of civilization. It is evident that this progress is not to be retarded by sneers, or calumnies, or the partisan interference of universities, or even by legislative injustice and persecution. The sentence, *Magna est veritas et prevalebit*, in this case strikes as much terror into the hearts of the upholders of old abuses, as the still more ancient judgment, *Mene*, *mene*, *tekel*, *upharsin*, when written by the finger of the Almighty on the walls of the Assyrian palace.

But what can the allopathists do? They are committed to a system; their daily bread or their luxurious life is dependent on its ascendancy; and they have no resort but at all hazards to oppose whatever may endanger its popularity or stability. And the history of dogmatic controversy furnishes no parallels for the uncandid, ungenerous, and altogether unworthy methods resorted to by the supporters of the *ancien régime*, in medicine, against the disciples of Hahnemann and the great masses of intelligent people who are induced by the constant successes which mark the advance of his theory to accept it as their law in cases of disease.

The first, the greatest of all difficulties in the way of a defence of the allopathic practice is, that that practice is not the result of a *system*. There is about it nothing of method, or proportion, nothing philosophical; but the whole collection of its propositions is admitted, by its most eminent professors, to be incongruous, uncertain, and entirely without any pervading and harmonizing idea. Undoubtedly the experience of two thousand years has been prolific of facts, but no one has ever pretended, from the chaotic accumulation, to call into life an orderly, symmetrical and philosophical system, to reduce the results of experience and observation in Allopathy to a *science.* Homœopathy has this great advantage, that, like Minerva, it sprang into existence perfect in its grand and beautiful symmetry, as complete in its parts and orderly in its movement as that universe of which the secret flashed upon the father of astronomy like a new and infinitely sublime creation.

The reception of Homœopathy has been in a singular degree parallel with the reception of other great truths, especially in the earlier years of their promulgation. The educated and thoughtful perceived their truth, or at least paused before rejecting it. The ignorant, incapable from intellectual weakness or perverse dispositions, rejected it with vulgar abuse and abortive wit. Our readers will perhaps all remember a dialogue between a homespun farmer and a young collegian, printed in some of the school books used a quarter of a century ago, in which the student is put down by logic something like what follows:

"*James.* What's that you say? this great masterly world is round, and turns round every day? You're a fool! The world's as flat as a pancake. Why if what you tell is the case, how happens it that all the water is n't spilt out of my mill-pond every night?"

Here was a show of logic, a show of wit; it was all very plausible to the objector, and to persons of his calibre; it is parallel with the opposition to the principle in medicine, *similia similibus curantur*, which is above the comprehensions of the vulgar, as it is destructive of the professional advantages and reputations of the adherents of the rapidly decaying practice of the immethodical, inconsistent, and dangerous traditional dogmas which it is destined to supersede.

The following chapters have been very hastily prepared, amid the anxieties of a most arduous professional occupation, but it will be found that they fully meet, and, it is trusted, satisfactorily answer the trivial criticisms and unscrupulous misstatements of an author who has chosen by exhibitions of audacity and a want of conscience to challenge such consideration as he would in vain attempt to secure by a legiti mate trial of his strength, in fair controversy.

A Roman matron being inquired of as to her

jewels, presented her children. We emulate the noble example of Cornelia; and although we have condescended for once to enter the lists with a Worthington Hooker, for the purpose of refuting his calumnies, we have far greater satisfaction in pointing to the numerous families in which the Hahnemannic practice is accepted, for demonstrations, in vigorous and unimpaired constitutions, of the truth of a system which preserves in their original beauty and power natures which a beneficent Creator designed for constant happiness and usefulness.

E. E. MARCY, M.D.

New-York, March 20, 1852.

CONTENTS.

CHAPTER I.

EXAMINATION OF ATTENUATED SUBSTANCES IN CONNECTION WITH ALLOPATHIC ARITHMETIC.

CHAPTER II.

FALLACIES OF DR. HOOKER CONCERNING DRUG PROVINGS.

CHAPTER III.

EXAMINATION OF THE HOMŒOPATHIC LAW OF CURE.

CHAPTER IV.

EXAMINATION OF DOCTRINES AND DOSES.

CHAPTER VII.

CONCLUDING OBSERVATIONS.

REPLY TO DR. HOOKER

ON

HOMŒOPATHY.

CHAPTER I.

EXAMINATION OF ATTENUATED SUBSTANCES IN CONNECTION WITH ALLOPATHIC ARITHMETIC.

Homœopathy has now been before the public for more than half a century. It has been introduced into every part of the civilized world; its principles have always been clearly announced, and wherever its practical value has been fairly tested, whether in public hospitals or in private practice, the results have uniformly demonstrated it to be more successful than any practice of medicine which has hitherto obtained. The system has, gradually, but steadily, continued to extend throughout the area of civilization, until it has enlisted among its earnest advocates a very large number of the most intelligent of every country. Attacked, and misrepresented as it has ever been, by the mercenary physicians and apothecaries of the Old School, it has still advanced triumphantly through all the storms of calumny, bitter invective, and malignant hate, which have been continually poured upon it. It will ever continue to advance until its momentous truths shall be universally recognised, and mankind be forever released from the blighting curse of Allopathy, and its death-dealing poisons.

Among the thousand and one attacks which have been made upon Homœopathy and its advocates, we have recently noticed one entitled, "*Homœopathy, an Examination into its Doctrines and Evidences, by Worthington Hooker, M. D.*" Like every other attack which has been made upon the system, it is a mere tissue of misrepresentations, and tricky artifices to mislead the ignorant and unthinking from its real doctrines, and to divert attention from the actual points at issue between the schools. With intelligent minds, such poor sophistries and silly attempts at "reviewing evidences," of course carry with them their own refutation, and recoil upon the heads of those whose cupidity or malice have prompted them to issue them. But as there is a class of persons who may possibly peruse this essay, under the supposition that it is an honest exposition of the Homœopathic doctrine, we shall take occasion to strip the author of the flimsy web with which he has invested himself, and display him to the world, a pettifogging perverter of facts, a calumniator of a large class of judicious scholars, who are his superiors in all respects, and a mere panderer to the hate, malice, and medical demagogism of the more contemptible of his school.

Like all other Allopathists who have written against Homœopathy, the gentleman from Connecticut, Dr. Worthington Hooker, has laid himself out on *infinitesimal doses*. As many have done before him, he has entered into mathematical calculations, of the high dilutions, and has attempted to be exceedingly witty upon the absurdity of supposing the existence of power in imponderable substances. Mark well the point, viz., Dr. Worthington Hooker, of Norwich, Connecticut, asserts that he cannot figure up the weight of the molecules of certain imponderable substances like the higher attenuations of Homœopathy, (he very shrewdly forgets to allude to other imponderables in the same connection, like miasmata, the contagious particles of smallpox, scarlet fever, measles, and certain forms of typhus, the atomic particles floating in the air of cholera-infected districts, magnetism, electricity, light, caloric, etc. etc.,) and therefore, that these imponderables must of necessity be powerless. The astute genius of Worthington Hooker, M. D., has figured it all out, and has demonstrated with perfect transparency, that Homœopathy is absurd, and that no one can reason upon medical topics but allopathic physicians, with intellects as penetrating as his own. It is granted that scientific men, clergymen, etc., may reason very logically upon all other topics but that of medecine; this is forbidden ground, because, in this field, their mental vision at once becomes perverted; allopathy appears to them like a grim and terrible monster, glutted with victims of two thousand years, and they turn instinctively to Homœopathy for relief to their sufferings.

Now, although we deny emphatically, that the subject of *doses* has any thing to do with the great homœopathic principle of cure, and while we assert that the selection of doses always has been and always will be subject to the judgment of the practitioner, who, whether he chooses a tincture or a dilution, may still be a consistent homœopath, we shall, however, take this close reasoning gentleman, Worthington Hooker, M. D., of Connecticut, as we find him, and show him that *imponderable* substances, yea, imponderable quantities of vegetable, animal, and mineral substances, are not so entirely inefficient in impressing the human body as he pretends to believe, but that they do possess powers, so wonderful and efficient in their character, that even his own comprehensive intellect can scarcely have a conception of their extent, much less of their mathematical, chemical, or physical properties. Before proceeding with this subject, we make the following quotations from the writer, to show that he was perfectly aware of the fact that even Hahnemann himself considered the question of infinitesimal doses a matter totally distinct from his great principle of cure, *similia similibus curantur*. Indeed, it is known by every student of medicine, that Hahnemann made use of medicines in the usual forms and doses for a considerable period after the announcement of his chief discovery, and it was only from experience and repeated experiments that he discovered the powers of small doses during disease. But to the quotation:

" I now invite the attention of the reader to an exposition of the system of Hahnemann, as developed in his 'Organon,' a work which is universally regarded, by homœopathists, as the great text-book of medicine" (page 15).

The writer here gives a summary of Hahnemann's conclusions, and then observes that, "in this summary, or analysis of the homœopathic method, (as he calls it) the reader will notice that there is nothing said about infinitesimal doses. And it is remarkable that there is not the slightest hint upon this subject in the Organon, till we reach the 204th page, though the whole book contains but 300 pages, and then it is alluded to only in a note, and that merely incidentally. Almost all he does say about it, from begining to end, is said in notes. In the text, it is not treated of at all in any explicit and circumstantial manner, but is barely hinted at" (page 20).

Why, then, in the name of reason, with these facts staring you in the face, have you taxed your calculating powers so enormously upon this "incidental" and unimportant point? Why have you not taken the "great text-book of the homœopath" as you found it, and criticized it *honestly* and *fairly*, instead of selecting a proposition which is only "barely hinted at in the Organon," to vent upon it your hatred against a rival school?

We take the liberty of calling into requisition once more the mathematical genius, the irresistible logic, and the wonderful acumen, of this shining light of Allopathy, who presents himself so confidently as its champion. We desire him to take into consideration the following substances, which "homœopaths, scientific men, clergymen, etc.," really believe to possess some power of action on the human body, and to describe to us their weight and bulk, as well as their chemical and physical characteristics. As the value or absurdity of all things is to be measured by the "plain common sense," and the vast comprehension of this Connecticut gentleman, will he hasten to enlighten us upon these subjects, so that we may no longer be deluded by absurd notions of such "loose reasoners" as Newton, Davy, Locke, Herschell, etc.?

1. It is well known that when vegetable substances are subjected to a certain amount of heat and moisture, the atoms or molecules of which they are composed are set free, and become diffused in infinitesimal proportions through the atmosphere, for miles in extent, so that any individual inhaling this air, will get a *dose* of these atoms of sufficent strength to poison his body, and cause intermittent fever. These are some of nature's high attenuations, and have been termed by medical writers, *miasmata.*

We beg leave to summon this quick oracle, whose 'close reasoning," and extraordinary mathematical, and chemical genius is destined to direct the judgments of "intelligent scientific men, clergymen, etc.," to display on this point all his calculating powers and to give us the weight in figures of a quantity of these miasmatic atoms sufficient to infect a large army, or if this puzzles him, the inhabitants of the whole universe, with intermittent fever; to inform us of some chemical test by which we may detect these atoms in the immense space throughout which they are diffused; to give us some tangible and comprehensible idea of their physical properties, so that we may really know that such things do exist as *miasmata*, and that they are not the mere fanciful imaginings of a "homœopath, a scientific man, or a clergyman!" Will he put them under the lens of his most powerful microscope, and instruct us "loose reasoners" respecting their size, shape, and general appearance?

What if such insignificant chemists as Lavoisier, Berzelius, Davy, Black, Dumas, and Faraday, have repeatedly attempted to detect chemically these miasmatic particles without success? doubtless these men were "loose reasoners," and were not blessed with the keen, analyzing powers of the gentleman from Norwich!

What if such intelligences as those of Newton, Euler, Dalton and Euclid could not, either by their own, or even "Homœopathic arithmetic," calculate their weight, dimensions, and shape, and therefore decided to consider and to call them imponderable, (*i. e.* having no weight,)—why, let it be remembered that Worthington Hooker, M.D., of Connecticut, was not then in existence!

What if those half-learned astronomers, Herschell and Chevalier, have no lenses sufficiently powerful to see these vegetable atoms—nature's homœopathic attenuations—does it follow that the keen sight of the Connecticut champion of Allopathy should not see them? Before his next essay appears, we may expect that he will put a dose of a high homœopathic attenuaation into one scale, and a dose of fever miasm into the other, and gravely inform us which sinks the beam.

But suppose the gigantic intellect of our critic should fail in all these tests—suppose his "arithmetic" stops short, and he becomes lost in a maze of miasms, what becomes of all the preconceived ideas upon this subject? Why they are swept, of course, by the dictum and "close reasoning" of this gordian master in logic, into instant annihilation. Can anything which *he* cannot "figure up," see, taste, smell, and handle, be aught else than a humbug—the offspring of fancy and "loose reasoning?" Wooden nutmegs and brass clocks forbid!

2. We again invoke the arithmetic and chemistry of this champion of crudities. In common with a large portion of the medical world, we deluded homœopaphists have always supposed that infinitesimal particles were constantly escaping from patients suffering from small-pox, scarlet fever, etc., and that these particles, when introduced into the blood through the lungs, were capable of contaminating the human organism with such maladies.

Here we beg the mathematical gentleman from Connecticut to bring again his wonderful "arithmetic" to bear, and give us some idea of the weight, or the chemical and physical properties of these contagious molecules? Or if the result should not tally with the standard of power, as inculcated by Worthington Hooker, M. D., of Connecticut—if with his arithmetic he cannot cypher out their weight and bulk, then let him with his mighty breath, blow the "absurd bubble" out of existence, as a humbug which can only entrap the "homœopath, the scientific man, and the clergyman." Weigh us out, we pray thee, a little small-pox contagion, if it be only a millionth, or even a sextillionth part of a grain! Or, if your arithmetic and scales are both out of order, give us some delicate chemical test, so that we may know that contagion and small-pox are not humbugs. Or, perhaps, it would be more agreeable to the gentleman to calculate the weight and bulk of another of nature's high attenuations—as, for example, the molecules of which the infection of Asiatic cholera is supposed to consist. Let us have the weight of all these molecules indeed which have existed since the world began, or we shall be obliged to consider them as "humbugs,"—mere phantasies of "homœopathists, scientific men, and clergymen!" Let no one commit the absurdity of supposing that any material substance can possess power, or in any way affect the human structures, unless its weight and dimensions can be accurately calculated in figures, by the "arithmetic" of Worthington Hooker, M. D., of Connecticut, the champion of modern Allopathy.

3. But it is possible, instead of displaying his "towering arithmetic" upon the infinitesimal particles of vegetable, animal, and mineral substances that he would prefer to "cypher" on material substances of a different class. As the recent experiments of Professor Andrew Crosse, in England, have conclusively demonstrated that water and other liquids can be so highly charged with electrical particles as to render them powerfully antiseptic when taken into the human stomach, as well as to give them new and potent chemical properties, will our phenomenon illuminate the world by a mathematical, chemical, and physical description of electrical molecules? We trust that

the "arithmetic" will prove successful, or electricity must henceforth be considered a "humbug," and all those old fashioned individuals who believe in it, like Franklin, Dufay, Priestley, Gay Lussac, Volta, Morse, and Page, must be ranked with those "deluded loose reasoners," the "homœopathists, scientific men, and clergymen." Come, O "close reasoning" champion of Allopathy, weigh us out the charge of electricity it would require to rend a world to fragments. You have presumed to reduce all phenomena within the scope and appreciation of your own infallible intellect —you, who deny the existence of power in attenuated atoms, unless you can see them, smell them, taste them, weigh them, and clutch them in your brawny hands, tell the "loose reasoning" and benighted world something about the physical qualities of these electrical molecules!

Would you prefer to experiment on the particles of matter which are continually escaping from the magnet? Baron Reichenbach, an allopathist, who has recently published a very learned work upon this subject, not only asserts that *magnetic atoms* continually escape from magnets in definite directions, but that these atoms may actually be *seen* in a dark room, by sensitive persons. We beg leave to ask the mathematical gentleman of Connecticut to reply in his next attack on homœopathy, to this reasonable query: Suppose a million, a billion, or a sextillion of the most powerful horseshoe magnets ever made, should be kept in full operation for a period dating from the creation of Adam to the probable final destruction of the world, and that all the magnetic atoms escaping them should be collected together, what, according to your "arithmetic," would be their weight and bulk?

If the gentleman from Norwich will take his compass and go to any part of the world, he will find the needle invariably pointing towards the magnetic pole, thus showing that the molecules which escape from this great magnetic deposit pervade the whole universe, exercising an attraction under all circumstances towards the parent source. At the pole itself, it was ascertained by Sir John Ross, that the needle uniformly points directly downward, or perpendicularly to the surface of the earth. At every other point on the globe, the needle forms some sort of an angle with the pole, unless affected by local causes. Will this monster of science inform us how much this universe of molecules weighs?

While our allopathic opponents are attempting to ridicule the idea of power in imponderable agents, and other phenomena which they cannot understand, and which their heathen idols, Hippocrates and Galen, forgot to teach, why do they not cry out, "humbug," against another mysterious and inexplicable force which has recently been introduced to the scientific world by Liebig and his cotemporaries, and which has been termed *catalysis?* Why do they not perpersuade some of their mathematical geniuses to "*cypher*" on the subject, so that we may comprehend the *rationale* of catalytic action?

Modern chemists have ascertained that the mere *contact* or *presence* of minute quantities of certain substances, with indefinitely large proportions of other substances, communicate to the latter entirely new and potent qualities. In this process the acting agent loses no appreciable weight and undergoes no apparent change, and yet results of the most important character are manifested.

"The active force in a compound," according to Liebig,* "depends on a certain order or arrangement, in which its elementary particles touch each other." "The chemical force of sulphuric acid is present in sulphate of lime as entire as in oil of vitriol. It is not appreciable by the senses; but if the cause be removed which prevented its manifestation, it appears in its full force in the compound in which it properly resides."

"In compounds of this kind, in which the free manifestation of the chemical force has been impeded by other forces, a blow, or *mechanical friction*, or the *contact of a substance*, the particles of which are in a state of motion (decomposition, transformation,) or any external cause, whose activity is added to the stronger attraction of the elementary particles in another direction, may suffice to give the preponderance to this strongest attraction, to overcome the *vis inertiæ*, to alter the form and structure of the compound, which are the result of foreign causes, and to produce the resolution of the compound into one or more new compounds with altered properties."

"In examples of this class, an infinite variety of new forces are developed from apparently inactive substances, by the invisible operation of elementary particles contained in these substances. Mere *friction* or *contact* of a small quantity of one substance

* Animal Chem., page 62.

with another, effects transformations and developes new properties in the latter without the slightest appreciable loss of weight, bulk, or chemical properties of the former.

"It is remarkable," says Kane, "that this law of catalysis, of which the simplest expression is, that where two chemical substances are in contact, any motion occurring among the particles of the one may be communicated to the particles of the other, is of a more purely mechanical nature than any other principle as yet received in chemistry; and when more definitely established by succeeding research, it may be the basis of a *dynamical theory in chemistry.*"

"We must, at least, look upon these actions of catalysis, as tending towards a change in our ideas of the nature of chemical affinity, which may before long remodel the whole constitution of the science."

We might extend our queries, and "put sums" *ad infinitum*, but knowing that there *are* limits, even to such comprehensive and analytic intellects as that of Worthington Hooker, M.D., of Norwich, Connecticut, we pause, for the present, for replies to those already offered.

But seriously, is not that man a pitiable object, who, at this enlightened period, has the presumption and folly to measure the powers and properties of substances by bulk and weight? When the most obtuse intellect, by moderate observation and reflection, *may see that nearly all of the most active and potent material agents with which we are acquainted are imponderable—absolutely incapable of being appreciated by any mathematical, chemical, or other material test—*

is it not singular that an individual, who is recognised as a member of a learned profession, can be found, who, coolly and over his own signature, attempts to convince the public that attenuated and imponderable substances are inert, powerless, and unworthy of consideration? While I am penning this very paragraph, an important communication is brought me from a distance of more than 1000 miles, in an instant of time, by a few imponderable atoms of electricity! Their function is accomplished, and they are dissipated, perhaps to take a prominent part in some living organism, or perchance to convey again, on their quick wings, some communication—perhaps to Worthington Hooker, M.D., of Norwich, Connecticut.

It is melancholy to witness the extent to which the prejudices of individuals will carry them when their interests are at stake. They find no difficulty in understanding and acknowledging that all classes of imponderables (except that class pertaining to homœopathy), whether originating from the animal, vegetable, or mineral kingdoms, are powerful morbific, remedial, and chemical agents, and they would no more think of bringing "arithmetic" to bear upon them, than of entering into a mathematical calculation to ascertain the weight of the "vital principle which presides over the operations of the body, in sickness and in health."

Men have ever been prone to measure every new discovery and every unusual phenomenon by existing knowledge, or by their own limited capacities, and to pronounce everything absurd and a "humbug" which they could not at once comprehend and appreciate.

The vast discoveries of Galileo, Columbus, Newton, Harvey, Jenner, and Fulton, were first laughed at by the world, and met with all kinds of silly falsehoods and inuendoes by the "*material headed*" pamphlet writers of different periods. And where stand now the authors of these discoveries, and where their pitiful revilers? When our own Fulton first announced the powers of steam as a propelling agent, his scheme was regarded as absurd, and he himself was denounced as a visionary madman! Now the name of Fulton is immortal, while those of his aspersers have long been sunk in oblivion beneath the contempt of the world. So, when the powers of imponderable agents shall have become universally acknowledged and appreciated, will such "material headed reasoners" as this champion of Allopathy sink into merited obloquy, or rather, absolute oblivion.

From the few examples which we have adduced, we think it will be evident to the meanest capacity that infinitesimal atoms of vegetable, animal, and mineral substances, when introduced into the human organism, are capable of producing effects of great importance, and of almost infinite variety. Whether these substances have been reduced to their condition of infinitesimal subdivision by a natural or an artificial process, can be a matter of no consequence, provided the attenuations are effectually accomplished in either instance.

Notwithstanding, however, the self-evident fact of the efficacy of imponderable quantities of matter, a fact which has been recognised by nearly all of the most eminent philosophers and chemists of the 18th and 19th centuries, we again deny most emphatically that it has any necessary connection with the great homœopathic law of cure, *similia similibus curantur.* The question of doses was a mere matter of experience on the part of Hahnemann, gradually acquired by a long series of observations, some time *after* the discovery and public announcement of the main doctrines of Homœopathy. Hahnemann witnessed and deplored the general routine of indiscriminate drugging, with mixtures composed of almost every variety of poison, and endeavored to lessen the evil and to attain more accuracy and certainty, by proving drugs on healthy persons, in order to ascertain their specific action, and then to prescribe them singly. Until the time of Hahnemann physicians had striven with each other for the palm of giving the largest quantities of drugs, the more powerful the better, without absolutely destroying their poor patients. The discoverer of homœopathy adopted the opposite course, and used all his sagacity to ascertain how small a quantity of medicine would suffice to cure a disease. In accomplishing this object, he had no hypothesis to sustain—no ancient heathen dogma to bolster up—no prejudices to gratify; but his sole objects were truth, and the welfare of his fellow creatures. Guided by such laudable motives, and uninfluenced by the jealousies and calumnies of professional rivals and interested apothecaries, he devoted his whole energies, mental and physical, to the accumulation of facts, with the view of establishing a rational system of medicine. How much he has done towards attaining his end, we leave for others to decide.

In perusing the mendacious attack of this Connecticut defamer, the uninformed reader is induced to suppose that he may be honest, and that he really aims to give the public a true representation of the homœopathic doctrine and its evidences. With a degree of hypocrisy which would do credit to the most shrewd Jesuit, and with a considerable amount of poor cunning, the author has selected a few isolated passages from the writings of Hahnemann, which have no bearing upon his doctrine of cure, and held them up as a "view of Homœopathy." He likewise professes to give a view of the system, as announced by other standard authors. Farther on we shall quote from these writers proofs of the entire lack of foundation for these assumptions.

CHAPTER II.

FALLACIES OF DR. HOOKER CONCERNING DRUG PROVINGS.

The second chapter of the "doctrines and evidences" is chiefly devoted to the provings of drugs, on persons in health, with reference to their application in disease, and to the "manner in which little doses cure."

The writer calls attention to the "manner in which homœopathists discover to what disease any remedy has that peculiar affinity, which is an essential condition of its curative power. It is done," he says, "in this way: the remedy is given to persons in health; the symptoms which follow in them are carefully and minutely noted down; after making out this group of symptoms, you may be sure, as they say, that in whatever case you find a similar group of symptoms, there you have the disease which this remedy, in infinitesimal doses, will cure."

In conducting these provings the writer asserts that there is "no formal set of rules prescribed, and that there is nothing very definite in regard to the *size* of the doses used." The utter absurdity of these assertions will of course be apparent to all who are in the slightest degree familiar with homœopathic writings;

but as they may be seen by some who are ignorant of the doctrines of Homœopathy, we deem it proper to refute them at the onset.

The present writer has personally beheld and perused a large number of original provings by Hahnemann, in his own handwriting, detailing minutely the circumstances under which the different drugs were taken, the *exact sizes* of the doses used, and the symptoms arising from these doses. All these facts are described by Hahnemann in their regular order, and with a systematic precision and minuteness unparalleled in such investigations. In these provings the drugs were employed both in the crude form, in large doses, and in an attenuated state, in order that their entire effects might thus be thoroughly displayed. Indeed we were repeatedly informed by Madame Hahnemann, the wife of the founder of our system, that her husband had often been made seriously ill for months at a time in consequence of his experiments with large doses of crude drugs. Nearly all of his earlier provings were made with crude medicines, in various doses; but afterwards reflecting that the efforts of nature are always directed to the speedy expulsion from the system of noxious substances, by vomiting, purging, or some other excretory process, he deemed it essential that small doses should also be employed, in order that they might be retained for a longer period, and thus afforded time to manifest their entire pathogeneses.

Hahnemann has always inculcated the importance of proving drugs, in both a crude and attenuated state, and in a variety of doses. In every proving which he or his disciples have ever made, these forms and doses have been most accurately specified, as the experiments advanced; but the impropriety of including all these details in a Materia Medica, and the impossibility of pointing out beforehand the exact quantity of each drug to be taken, in a work like the Organon, will be apparent to every man of common sense. The rules which we find in the Organon are as precise as can be embraced in any work of this character, as the following quotations will show :—

"Thus there is no safer or more natural method of discovering the effects of medicines on the health of man than by trying them, separately and singly, in moderate doses, upon *healthy* individuals, and observing what changes they create in the moral and physical state; that is to say, what elements of disease these substances are capable of producing."—(Organon, p. 136.)

"In studying the effects of medicines upon healthy persons, it must not be forgotten that even the administration of moderate doses of the so-called heroic remedies is sufficient to produce modifications in the health of the most robust individuals. Medicines that are more gentle in their nature ought to be given in larger doses if we would likewise prove their action. Finally, if we would try the effects of the weakest substances, the experiment must be made upon persons only who are, it is true, free from disease, but who, at the same time, are possessed of a delicate, irritable and sensitive constitution."—(Organon, p. 142.)

"Each of these medicines ought to be taken in its

simple and pure form. As to indigenous plants, the juice is expressed and mixed with a small quantity of alcohol, in order to preserve it from corruption. With regard to foreign plants they are to be pulverized or prepared as spirituous tinctures, and mixed with a certain quantity of water previous to administration. Salts and gums, however, ought not to be dissolved in water till the moment they are to be used. If a plant cannot be procured but in its dry state, and if its powers are naturally feeble, it may be tried in the form of an infusion; that is to say, after having cut it up small, boiling water is poured upon it in order to extract its virtues. The infusion ought to be drunk immediately after its preparation, and while it is still warm, because all the juices of plants, and all vegetable infusions to which no alcohol is added, pass rapidly into fermentation and corruption, and thereby lose their medicinal virtues."—(Organon, p. 143.)

"Sometimes a person apparently delicate is not at all affected by a medicine that is known to be very powerful, though administered in moderate doses, while other substances that are much weaker make a tolerable impression on him. At the same time there are individuals of robust constitutions who experience very considerable morbid symptoms from medicinal agents that are apparently mild, and, on the other hand, they are likewise but little affected by others that are powerful. But as it can never be known beforehand which of these two cases will occur, it is proper that each should commence with a small dose, and be afterwards increased progressively if deemed requisite. Advancing, from day to day, to higher and still higher doses."—(Organon, p. 145.)

So far then as the provings of Hahnemann are concerned, although they were chiefly made some forty years ago, when Homœopathy was in its infancy, it is evident that the statements and inferences published by Dr. Hooker are utterly false and contemptible. The writer even contradicts himself upon this point as he does upon many others. On page 33, he remarks in regard to the provings that "there is no formal set of rules prescribed, and we are left to *infer* for the most part what the principles are which govern observers in conducting these 'provings,' as they are termed."

On page 51, we find, "All agree as to the mode of conducting the provings."

We have personally seen and examined carefully the greater part of Hahnemann's original manuscripts, which are still in possession of his wife, at Paris, and can therefore vouch for the several facts to which we have alluded.

In regard to the vast number of provings made by the disciples of Hahnemann, within the last fifty years, we have only to remark, that it is a fact perfectly well known to those who have taken any pains to investigate the subject, that in all instances the doses have been specified, the symptoms have been carefully noted as they occurred, and all circumstances connected with the experiments have been minutely detailed.

With reference to the symptoms which have been adopted into our Materia Medica, the following course has been pursued:

1. A careful collection of symptoms which have been observed in cases of accidental or intentional poisoning, with the pathological appearances present in those who have died from the effects of drugs.

2. A selection of such symptoms as have been repeatedly experienced from a given drug, in large and small doses, by many different provers, in different parts of the world.

3. Symptoms derived from reliable Allopathic sources.

4. Symptoms which have been repeatedly dissipated by remedies selected in accordance with the law of *similia similibus curantur.*

One would naturally suppose that a Materia Medica founded on such data as these, should be entitled to some confidence. Sustained as our provings are, by such a variety of self-evident facts, one might believe that it would require a man of much more than ordinary impudence and recklessness, to call these provings imaginary and fictitious.

But the writer does not find fault alone with the manner of conducting the provings; he would strike down the whole system of experimenting with drugs, in health, as useless. In other words, instead of ascertaining the true specific effects of single drugs by actual experiments upon the human body, in order that they may be prescribed with some degree of certainty in disease, he would have us believe that it is more philosophical to prescribe them at random—mixed together in strange confusion, and without any knowledge of their specific action, in accordance with the instructions of the alchemists and other practitioners who flourished during the dark ages. The idea of administering medicines *singly*, and in a pure form, is supposed to be particularly absurd and unscientific, and is sneered at accordingly. So thought those respectable ancients who founded Allopathy, and who deemed it essential to mix together as many articles as possible in one prescription, in order that some one of them should hit the disease! One very scientific modern Allopathic physician had a favorite recipe consisting of 100 different ingredients of every possible description; like opiates, cathartics, tonics, antiphlogistics, stimulants, sedatives, acids, alkalis, etc., all mixed together with the most perfect disregard of every chemical or other rule. His argument was, that "out of so many dissimilar and potent drugs, there must surely be one which would hit the nail on the head and cure the malady."

The same theory is now practically adopted by the great body of Allopathists. They scout the idea of ascertaining the pure effects of medicines upon the human organism, but prefer random shots with a great number of articles, with different properties. By this course, they are pretty sure to hit the patient effectually, whether the disease is reached or not.

We have the pleasure, however, of recording the truth, that many distinguished Allopathists have, in late years fully recognised the importance of drug provings on the healthy, as a guide to their application in disease. Such facts are of course bitter pills for such medical bigots as Dr. Hooker, but we proceed to administer them, as follows:

Professor Dunglison, in his work on "New Remedies," page seventh, writes thus: "To treat disease methodically and effectively, the nature of the actions of the living tissues, in both the *healthy* and *morbid* conditions, must be correctly appreciated; the effects which the articles of the Materia Medica are capable of exerting under both those conditions, must be known from accurate observation, and not until then can the practitioner prescribe with any well founded prospect of success."

Dr. Paris, in his Materia Medica, remarks that "observation and experiment upon the effects of medicine are liable to a thousand fallacies, unless they are carefully repeated under the various circumstances of *health* and *disease*, in different climates, and on different constitutions."

Pereira assures us, "that in order to ascertain the action of remedial agents on the living body, it is necessary that we examine their influence both in *healthy* and *diseased* conditions. For, by the first we learn the positive or actual power of a medicine over the body; while by the second, we see how that power is modified by the presence of disease." (Per. Mat. Med. and Ther., vol. 1, p. 126.)

The justness of these observations will be instantly recognised by every man of common sense and common honesty. The intolerant and ignorant aspersers of Hahnemann, will continue, as a matter of course, to vent their angry spite against this as well as his other reformations, but their simple declamation will, as heretofore, be disregarded.

CHAPTER III.

EXAMINATION OF THE HOMŒOPATHIC LAW OF CURE.

In this chapter Dr. Hooker professes to "examine the *doctrines* of Homœopathy;" and it is here that he displays, in a most pitiable manner, his utter ignorance of the whole system as taught by Hahnemann and his followers. For example, he says "if the doctrine, *similia similibus curantur* be the *sole* law of therapeutics, the totality of effects produced by any article in the healthy, should be a sure indication that this article will relieve a similar set of symptoms whenever they appear in the sick. For example, opium produces in the healthy a state of insensibility and somnolency, and ipecac. produces nausea and vomiting. Therefore, if the homœopathic law be the sole law of cure, opium should invariably relieve insensibility and somnolency in the sick, and ipecac. should invariably relieve nausea and vomiting. It matters not that they *sometimes* do this in some particular cases: to prove the law to be the *sole* law they should *always* do it." (p. 54.)

According to the writer's own confession a remedy in order to be truly homœopathic in disease, must be selected which will cover the *totality* of the symptoms. In other words that that medicine alone is homœopathic, which produces in the healthy a totality of symptoms closely resembling those of the disease to be cured. Suppose then we have a case of insensibility and somnolency, with a dozen other important symptoms which opium *does not* produce in the healthy, does opium correspond to this *totality* of symptoms, and is it perfectly homœopathic in this instance? If the totality of the symptoms consists *only* of insensibility and somnolency, like that which opium produces when taken in health, then will opium most assuredly cure, and that too "invariably."

Ipecac. "invariably" cures nausea with eructations, and accumulation of saliva in the mouth during the nausea, and vomiting of mucus or the ingesta, because it produces these symptoms in the healthy; but it does not always cure nausea and vomiting, attended with violent pains in the stomach, internal burning heat, intense thirst, dryness of the mouth and throat, and great tenderness of the stomach on pressure, because these symptoms are *not* caused by ipecacuanha when taken in health. In this case, arsenicum corresponds to the totality of symptoms, because it does produce these symptoms in the healthy, and it will therefore cure.

For cases of nausea and vomiting accompanied by different trains of symptoms, such as neither of the above medicines produce in health, other drugs, which will accurately correspond to these groups, will alone prove efficacious.

"Beyond the totality of the symptoms there is nothing discoverable in diseases by which they could make known the nature of the medicines they stand in need of, and we ought therefore to conclude naturally that there can be *no other indication* whatever than the *ensemble* of the symptoms in each individual case to guide us in the choice of a remedy." (Organon, p. 86.)

This language is clear and explicit. It is not by one or two symptoms of a disease that we are to be guided in the selection of the appropriate remedy, but by the *ensemble*—the grand total.

This is the doctrine inculcated by Hahnemann, and if Dr. Hooker had given the subject ordinary attention, he would never have advanced so "shallow and contemptible" an argument against it.

Further on we find the following: "If *similia similibus curantur* be the sole law of cure, then a remedy should never produce in the sick effects similar to those which it produces in the healthy."

In making this observation it is quite evident either that the writer has *intentionally* endeavored to deceive his reader, or that he has never read the Organon or the other works, with which he professes to be familiar. Had he consulted these works he would have learned that it is a fundamental principle of the homœopathic theory and practice, to create with the medicine an *artificial* disease similar to the *natural* one, but a little stronger, for a brief period, which shall supersede and annihilate it. He would have learned further that natural diseases are prone to run on until disorganization occurs—the reactive forces of the system exercising comparatively little influence over them; while medicinal diseases, when not excessive, are temporary, and yield readily to the recuperative powers of the organism. He would also have learned that drugs produce *primitive* and *secondary* effects, the first of which, in the case of homœopathic remedies, are like the natural disease, but of short duration; while the last are of a character directly *opposite*, or *curative*, and permanent.

"Every agent that acts upon the human economy, every medicine produces more or less some notable change in the existing state of the vital powers, or creates a certain modification in the health of man for a period of shorter or longer duration; this change is called the *primitive effect.* Although this is the joint effect of both a medicinal and a vital power, it belongs, notwithstanding, more particularly to the former, whose action is exercised upon the body. But our vital powers tend always to oppose their energy to this influence or impression. The effect that results from this, and which belongs to our conservative vital powers and their automatic force, bears the name of *secondary effect* or *reaction.*"

"So long as the primitive effects of artificial morbific agents (medicines) continue their influence upon a healthy body, the vital power appears to play merely a passive part, as if it were compelled to undergo the impression of the medicine that is acting upon it from without. But, subsequently, this also appears in a manner to rouse itself. Then, if there exists any state directly contrary to the primitive effect, the vital power manifests a tendency to produce one that is proportionate to its own energy, and the degree of influence exercised by the morbid or medicinal agent; and if there exists no state in nature that is directly contrary to this primitive effect, the vital power then seeks to gain the ascendancy by destroying the change that has been operated upon it from without (by the action of the medicine), for which it substitutes its own natural state (*reaction*)."

"For example, somnolence and stupor are *primitive effects* of opium, which continue ten, twelve, or more hours, according to the size of the dose; sleeplessness and nervous excitement always succeed this state, constituting the *secondary effect* of the drug." "Constipation, excited by opium (primitive effect), is followed by diarrhœa (secondary effect); and evacuations produced by purgatives (primitive effect), are succeeded by costiveness which lasts several days (secondary effect). It is thus that the vital power, in its reaction, opposes to the primitive effects of strong doses of medicine which operate powerfully on the healthy state of the body, a condition that is *directly opposite*, whenever it is able to do so."

"It is true that even small doses produce primitive effects that are perceptible; but the reaction made by the living organism never exceeds the degree that is requisite for the re-establishment of health." (Organon, p. 112–13.)

The homœopath, therefore, always attacks the disease itself, by producing with his remedies, such impressions upon the *disordered structures* as shall annihilate the original morbid action, and substitute in its stead a temporary drug action, which the recuperative forces of the system always speedily remove, if the malady be curable. The causes of disease are, for the most part, subtile, imponderable, and in many instances absolutely immaterial, like sudden news, grief, fright, anger, and other mental emotions; and it is not surprising that infinitesimal doses of drugs, when properly selected, may uniformly operate in such a manner as to overcome these first causes, and occupy their places. In effecting his object, the homœopath sometimes produces a temporary aggravation of symptoms with his remedy, but this is always of short duration, and is invariably followed by a curative and permanent reaction of the system against the effects of the drug, which supersedes the disturbed equilibrium, and secures health. But if a sufficiently small dose of the medicine be employed, this aggravation, or *primitive effect*, will be nearly, and perhaps entirely imperceptible, and the curative reaction, or *secondary effect*, will commence almost immediately.

By experimenting with drugs in health, the homœopath knows precisely upon what structures they act specifically, and what symptoms they produce. He knows that disease, irritation, inflammation, and nervous erethism, render the tissues affected morbidly sensitive to impressions of all kinds, so that things which were salubrious and agreeable in health become then sources of the most exquisite pain, and often actually intolerable. He knows that if brandy, or meat, or condiments, be introduced into an inflamed stomach, the life of the patient is endangered. He knows if he exposes a patient with ophthalmia to the bright sunlight, or permits him to read and write by gaslight, that disorganization and loss of sight will be likely to ensue. In a word, he knows that nearly all diseases render the parts affected so extremely susceptible to impressions of every kind, that even infinitesimal doses of specific medicines produce manifest primitive effects, and therefore if he administers his remedies in a crude state, he is almost certain to produce too violent effects, in the forms of medicinal aggravations, like those which Hahnemann first observed from the use of ordinary doses of crude drugs. From *necessity*, therefore, and not from theory, the believer in Homœopathy uses small doses, in order to avoid the most serious medicinal actions. In regard to the doses, one rule obtains among all judicious homœopathists, viz.: to give a sufficient quantity of the drug to cure the disease, with as little detriment to the healthy parts, and to the general system, as possible. The homœopath has medicines of every grade of strength, from the saturated tinctures and alkaloids to the highest dilutions; but as he has to deal with morbid conditions, totally different from those in health, and with inflamed tissues, so refined in sensibility that light, noise, or even mental emotions, become powerful disturbing agents, he finds it necessary, from experience, to adapt his doses to the altered sensibility of the disordered parts, that he may avoid unnecessarily active influences. Is not this philosophical, reasonable, and perfectly in accordance with common sense?

If allopathists, with their empirical, contradictory, and pernicious notions, choose to combat diseases by inflaming healthy parts, and filling the systems of their patients with large quantities of deleterious drugs, of which they know nothing with certainty, *and which they never presume to take themselves, when sick*, we can only say, God help the poor victims, their patients! If they prefer to adhere to a school which has no fixed principles of theory or practice; a school which has successively adopted for a time, and then abandoned as worthless, more hypotheses and modes of treatment than could be even enumerated in a volume; a school abounding in professors who nearly all differ in opinion, (both theoretically and practically,) and who very generally quarrel when called together in consultation; a school eminently ill defined, unsuccessful, and which is entirely destitute of the confidence of many of its own most learned and accomplished adherents—we can only say, God is kind to them, in rendering their reminiscences of practice oblivious!

Among the numerous theoretical and practical tenets which have been in vogue in this school, we quote the following from a "*Practice of Physic, or Dr. Sydenham's Processus Integri, translated out of Latin into English, with large Annotations, Animadversions and Practical Observations on the Same*, by William Salmon, M. D. London: 1707." And let it be remembered that Sydenham was not only a standard allopathic author at the date of this performance, but that he *now* ranks as one of the fathers of Allopathy, whose name and memory are held in veneration by its modern disciples. Whether the latter have really improved upon their illustrious predecessor is a matter of doubt, which future generations will have to decide. Selecting the chapter on *Pleurisy* as a fair sample of the book, we present the writer's views respecting the cause of the malady, which he says consists of a "preternatural fermentation of the blood extravasated; in which fermentation, the sharp particles do by their points or acrimony, vellicate the membraceous parts, and being intimately fixed in the nervous fibres, they make a concussion therein, which because it is continued to the origination of the nerves, a sad sensation or pain does arise, which is various, dull, pungent, rending, throbbing, distending, corroding, &c., according to the nature of the part affected, quality of the spirits, and concurrent particles of the blood and humors" (page 52).

In regard to the treatment of Pleurisy, we quote the following from page 53: "Bleed on the affected side three or four times, and take away ten ounces of blood. The juice expressed out of *horse-dung*, with water drawn from *ox*, *calves*, *sheep*, or *hog's blood*, is commended as an excellent thing, because it imbibes the pleuritic acid. *Helmont* rejects bleeding as an accursed remedy; because a pleurisy, cured by bleeding, often leaves a consumption behind it; and that they who use bleeding much do often fall into this disease: He commends *powder of stag's tail*, which may be drank to a drachm at a time; so also *goat's blood*, taken liquid and warm, or dried and given in powder to a drachm or more. Powder of *bull's tail* is also good, and of a *boar's tooth*. Or, take *powder of goat's blood, and of stag's tail, of each one scruple; red poppy-water an ounce and a half; mix for a dose. Or, take flowers of red poppies, and of daisies, leaves of wild chicory, of each a handful; horse-dung an ounce and a half; boil in barley water a sufficient quantity*, strain, and *sweeten with syrup of red poppies:* of which let the sick take a draught now and then." Various other remedies are advised to cure this complaint, like the "*spirit, or volatile salt of man's blood, and of vipers, crab's eyes, etc.*," which are recommended as "*incomparable things*."

This, it is true, is the allopathy of 1707, but as the chief argument which at the present day is adduced in favor of the school, is *its antiquity*, and the great mass of facts, and of theoretical and practical observations, which have been handed down in it from the venerated fathers of Allopathy, it would be unfair to leave the doctrines of these periods unrepresented.

But, what real improvements has modern Allopathy made over ancient Allopathy? Are the *violent* and heterogeneous compounds of the moderns any more successful in curing diseases, than the more *harmless* compounds of the ancients? Are the random and haphazard formulæ of the one any more definite and satisfactory in their effects, than those of the other? Is the "volatile spirit of vipers, or of man's blood" any less indicated in pleurisy, than the "spirits of nitre, or of minderiri?" Are the powders of "stag's tail, boar's tooth, goat's blood, and crab's eyes," any less efficient in combatting this malady than Dover's powders, James's powders, and calomel powders? If we may believe the published reports of old allopathists, their treatment was more successful than that of their modern descendants; upon the principle, probably, that their remedies opposed fewer obstacles to the kindly operation of the *vis medicatrix naturæ*, than do those of young Allopathy. Will Dr. Hooker, and his confrères of 1852, with their spirits of nitre and minderiri, and their powders of calomel, opium, etc., pretend to cure pleurisy as speedily and as safely, as did Dr. Sydenham and his associates of 1700, with "spirits of vipers and of man's blood," and "powders of stag's tail, boar's tooth, and crab's eyes?" So far as we can ascertain the facts in the case, the balance of evidence is in favor of the old practice, and on all his own principles, we may insist on its adoption by Dr. Hooker.

At page 56, our candid and logical critic intimates that "Hahnemann and his followers assert most stoutly, that camphor removes the totality of symptoms called cholera." Where, among the writings of Hahnemann and his followers, has Dr. Hooker ever seen any assertion of this kind? Where can he point to a single passage from which even an inference might be drawn, that camphor *alone* covers and removes all the symptoms of cholera? In what homœopathic work has he ever seen it advised, except for certain specified symptoms, which may or may not be present in cholera?

Here again, Dr. Hooker has either made a wilful misrepresentation of the doctrines of Homœopathy, or he has never read the books he professes to criticize. Neither Hahnemann nor his disciples, have ever prescribed for the *name* of a disease, but always for *symptoms* alone. Camphor produces in the healthy a few symptoms which frequently, but not invariably, occur during certain stages of cholera; and it is for these symptoms alone that it is a specific remedy, and not for cholera as a unit, or a "totality of symptoms." Every one who has ever looked into a homœopathic work on practice, is perfectly aware that there are quite a number of remedies not less important than camphor, in the treatment of cholera, and that these remedies are always selected in accordance with the *symptoms* present in any given case. The most charitable construction, therefore, which can be put upon this part of the "examination of the doctrines of Homœopathy," would be of ignorance and stupidity on the part of the writer.

Again, on page 56, Dr. Hooker remarks: "If *similia similibus curantur* be the *sole* law under which cures are effected, then we should be able to prove, either that the vital powers are never competent to cure disease alone and unassisted by remedies, or, that they do it in conformity with the homœopathic law."

By referring to a quotation from Hahnemann* on page 112-13, the reader will at once appreciate the sophistry of this mode of reasoning. Hahnemann everywhere declares that there is always a reaction of the vital principle against *all* deleterious influences acting upon the body, whether morbific or medicinal; and that it is through the instrumentality of this *reaction* alone that cures are effected. It is true that morbific influences are often so intense in their effect as to resist the natural curative reaction of the vital force; and it is in cases of this kind that *new* medicinal impressions must be created in the place of the natural disease, in order that the vital powers may react successfully and thus induce a cure. If the morbific action has been slight this natural reaction will be sufficient to restore the disordered tissues to health; but if the action be more intense it must be changed to a healthy medicinal action before a cure can take place.

* Organon.

After commenting upon the fallacy of trusting to hypotheses and theories in founding a system of medical practice—*a course which has been pursued up to the present moment by allopathists*—the writer proceeds: "Not only is it untrue that *similia similibus curantur* is the *sole* law of therapeutics, but there is no proof that it is even one among the many laws of cure which are employed in the removal of disease."

If Dr. Hooker will examine the standard authors of Allopathy he will find that opium and alcoholic stimulants, when used to excess by the healthy, produce *delirium tremens;* and if he continues his examination he will see that these are the chief allopathic remedies for the cure of that disease. If Dr. Hooker will swallow an allopathic dose of rhubarb in health, he will experience, in a few hours, a perturbation in his bowels, attended by copious, loose evacuations, with a sour smell, etc.; if he consults his books he will observe that rhubarb is highly commended for diarrhœas of this character. If Dr. Hooker will drug himself for some time with mercury he will get an ulcerated mouth and throat, pains in his bones, foul breath, augmented sensibility of the body, etc.; if he again consults his books he will see that mercury is the only specific advised for the same group of symptoms which arise from syphilis. If Doctor Hooker will experiment upon himself with 30 or 40 grains of ipecacuanha, he will probably feel a nausea at the stomach which will cause him to expel the article with profound indignation; his allopathic authorities will inform him that this drug, in doses of one-sixth of a grain, is one of the most important remedies to cure nausea and vomiting. If Dr. Hooker will take large and repeated doses of balsam copaibæ in health he will experience symptoms quite similar to gonorrhœa: can he ever have heard of this as an allopathic remedy for that malady? Calomel, in repeated allopathic doses, causes, according to Pereira, dark or greenish mucus, and bloody stools, with griping and tenesmus: is there any medicine more frequently used by old-school practitioners to cure these symptoms than calomel? Topical applications to the healthy urethra of a strong solution of nitrate of silver give rise to symptoms which can scarcely be distinguished from gonorrhœa: if Dr. Hooker consults his "Ricord" he will find that this is the most prominent local remedy for the cure of that disorder. This same homœopathic law of *similia* applies with full force to the topical treatment now so generally adopted by allopathists for the cure of diseases of the mucous membranes of the throat and bronchia, and of the utero-genital structures.

We might multiply such examples *ad infinitum*, and prove, from the best old-school authorities, not only that these homœopathic remedies produce in health *symptoms similar* to those which they cure, but that they give rise to pathological changes similar to those caused by the action of natural diseases. Those who are familiar with the physiological researches of Flourens, Majendie, Brodie, Müller and Wilson, with reference to the specific operations of opium, belladonna, mercury, stramonium, alcohol, etc., upon men and animals, will at once recognise the truth of these remarks.

From the few examples just enumerated, in which our opponents employ the homœopathic law of cure, it is quite evident that they *practically* recognise its truth. Indeed, some allopathic writers, "taking the bull by the horns," concede its importance as a therapeutic law, and claim it as a discovery of Hippocrates. Not so, however, with the vindictive conservatives of the school, who cannot, or rather will not, see any proofs in science, except such as have the very mold of antiquity about them. These redoubtable oracles are regular descendants of the wise doctors who for so long a period and with such virulence ridiculed the discoveries of Harvey and Jenner.

In one part of his essay Dr. Hooker denounces "provings" of all kinds, and seeks to ridicule the minute directions given by Hahnemann for conducting them; and in referring to them again, on page 65, he dilates upon the importance of minuteness and precision, and informs us how in his opinion they should be managed. It is amusing to observe the grave assurance with which he writes of the "loose reasoning" and "loose analogies" of Hahnemann, who was so pre-eminently a man of facts, accurate in his data and logical in his deductions, and who has elicited the highest encomiums from men like Hufeland and Forbes for his genius and metaphysical acumen. It is certainly very laughable to behold a man of Dr. Hooker's calibre seeking to pit himself against an intellectual giant like Hahnemann; to see his few senseless phrases thrown at the great structure of Homœopathy, with about as much effect as a ragged urchin would produce in storming Castle Garden with snowballs; and then to suppose that his misrepresentations and flimsy sophistries will have the least weight or effect with any one in the wide world, if we except those allopathic physicians whose ideas and whose reasonings lie in their pockets. It is easy for an ape to chatter and make up faces at a lion, or for a cur dog to bark at the moon; and it is not difficult for small men to cry out continually, "quack," "impostor," "cheat," or to sustain these demolishing "arguments" by making mouths at the greatest and best of mankind.

When it is remembered that nearly every drug contained in the homœopathic Materia Medica has been repeatedly proved, in every variety of form and dose, by numerous medical men in various parts of the world, with uniform results, and that the pathological changes which have been observed by allopathists in those who have been poisoned by these drugs, fully confirm the records of provings, no candid man can doubt their truthfulness and reliability. Some of the provers have sacrificed health, comfort, and years of time, in such hazardous and laborious investigations, which will ever stand recorded as undying monuments of honor to these practical ameliorators of human danger and suffering. Indolent individuals who have themselves accomplished nothing in the field of science, and who lack the energy or talent to appreciate the works of others, may look wise and cry out "humbug and delusion!" but the great public, who are guided by facts and results, notwithstanding all mercenary attempts to mislead, will receive the truth and be benefitted accordingly.

CHAPTER IV.

EXAMINATION OF DOCTRINES AND DOSES.

In his fourth chapter, Dr. Hooker *again* throws himself into an extraordinary state of indignation respecting homœopathic doses. He is exceedingly provoked that homœopaths generally recognise different degrees of susceptibility in the sick organism, and that they have the obstinacy to select medicines of such strength as may appear most appropriate to induce a cure speedily and safely.

He observes, at page 72, "if medicines produce in infinitesimal doses such effects as are attributed to them, and if there be such wide differences in the susceptibilities of the sick, it must be very important to fix upon exactly the right dose in each case. And if an infinitesimal dose of a medicine, carefully prepared, with just the right amount of agitation and trituration, be appropriate to a case, then it would certainly be very injurious to the patient to give a million of such doses at once."

The shallowness and sophistry of this entire extract renders a refutation almost superfluous, as will be evident to all who reflect upon the operation of morbific substances upon the human body. Thus, a single inhalation of the atmosphere of a room infected with infinitesimal atoms of smallpox or scarlet fever contagion, is capable of giving rise to either of these maladies in their full force: according to Dr. Hooker, "a million of such inhalations" ought to demolish the unfortunate breathers! A small particle of the virus of chancre, or of a smallpox pustule, placed upon a denuded surface, produces the syphilitic ulcer or the variolous pustule, with all its attendant symptoms, but according to the "logical and close-reasoning" Dr. Hooker, a million times this amount of virus placed upon an exposed part, ought instantly to convert the strongest man into a "grease-spot." An individual passing rapidly through a marshy district infected with infinitesimal miasmatic atoms, becomes affected with intermittent fever: according to the philosophical critic, should this individual by chance be detained in this infected region for several weeks, he would get an intermittent fever of such awful intensity that he would evaporate into thin air by spontaneous combustion, or else be converted into a human icicle from the severity of his chills!

But it is unnecessary to multiply examples to show the absurdity of the modes of reasoning adopted by our disingenuous opponents. If they would devote but a tithe of that time to a candid and honest investigation of the great truths of the homœopathic doctrine, which they now expend in racking their brains to raise false issues and to invent sophistries and calumnies against it, they might perhaps meet with some degree of respect from the public, instead of that contempt which they now receive.

If these gentlemen will really examine the doctrines of Homœopathy, they will find among them the following plain and incontrovertible precepts:

1. The conservative forces of the organism are always brought to bear against all deleterious influences acting upon the tissues. If the disturbing cause be slight, nature alone suffices to bring about a curative reaction; but when the morbific impression is so intense as to resist the restorative efforts of nature, the homœopath deems it necessary to call in the aid of medicines.

2. In his remedial measures the homœopath recognises but one law of cure, viz., *similia similibus curantur*. But while he distinctly avows this doctrine so far as the application of drugs is concerned, he nowhere asserts, as Dr. Hooker falsely pretends, that the restorative efforts of nature are not alone sufficient, in many cases, to cure disease.

3. The only real cures ever made by drugs, are accomplished in accordance with the homœopathic law, whether made by physicians of the old or the new school—by crude drugs or by dilutions.

4. No two diseases, whether morbific or medicinal, can affect the same structure at the same time.

5. The vital force reacts with much less power against impressions made by morbific agents, than against those caused by specific medicinal influences. Disorders, therefore, caused by the former, tend to run on to the disorganization of the affected parts,

while those produced by the latter, speedily result in spontaneous recoveries.

6. Homœopathic medicines expend their entire forces upon those parts alone which are actually diseased; and it is for this reason that very minute doses are adequate to produce those impressions which result in spontaneous curative reactions.

7. A medicinal action, sufficient to cure disease, may be produced either by the tincture or by a dilution of the appropriate remedy,—our only object being, to substitute a healthy drug action in the place of a morbid one. Experience, however, has amply demonstrated, that in a majority of instances diluted drugs act more mildly, more speedily and more safely in provoking curative reactions, than crude medicines, the first impressions of which are more active than is absolutely necessary for curing, although not usually so active as to give rise to serious results.

Drugs never loose their identity, individuality, or specific modes of action, whatever may be the form they are made to assume. The word dose is a relative term, depending upon the nature and form of the drug, the sensitiveness of the patient, and the amount of inflammation or nervous erethism present in each case. If one grain of tartar emetic in solution, or twenty grains of ipecacuanha be introduced into a vein of one of the extremities of a healthy individual, the specific effects of these drugs upon the stomach and skin, will speedily become manifest by vomiting and perspiration. If $\frac{1}{30}$th of a grain of tartar emetic, or one half a grain of ipecac. be injected into the blood of the same individual their specific actions will still be maintained, although neither vomiting nor perspiration will be produced. But if the stomach or skin be affected with inflammation, or other morbid sensibility, the last named doses will then manifest their entire specific action in the form of nausea, vomiting, sweat, etc. If a given dose of medicine were administered to one hundred individuals, it is probable that no two of them would be affected with precisely the same symptoms; although the characteristic specific impressions of the drug would be produced in all, with different degrees of intensity. It is for this reason that homœopathists, from the time of Hahnemann to the present day, have employed, in their provings of drugs, every variety of form and dose, and numerous experimenters of different ages, sexes, temperaments, countries, and occupations, in order that the most complete pathogeneses might be obtained.

The susceptibilities of the tissues of the organism to medicinal impressions, are proportionate to the amount of inflammation, irritation, or nervous erethism present in each case; and as no two maladies or groups of symptoms ever correspond precisely in all respects, it follows that a great variety of strengths may be employed with advantage in our remedial applications.

10. In regard to doses, the homœopath has but one object in view, viz., the selection of that strength or attenuation which will most safely, mildly and speedily cure the disease. As this is purely a matter of experience and of facts, and not at all connected with the homœopathic theory of cure, its entire

reasonableness must commend itself to the judgments of candid men.

Let us now briefly contrast these homœopathic precepts with those generally adopted by our Allopathic opponents in the treatment of disease, and see on which side reason and truth lie.

Homœopathy addresses her remedies to those parts alone which are actually diseased: Allopathy, in her remedial measures, operates upon parts which are healthy.

Homœopathy seeks to cure disease with as little medicine as possible, in order that the organism shall not suffer from serious medicinal diseases: Allopathy employs enormous quantities of poisonous drugs for the express purpose of creating artificial diseases in healthy parts.

Homœopathy prescribes only for symptoms which really exist: Allopathy prescribes for various groups of symptoms under the same general name.

Homœopathy employs only those medicines which have been carefully and repeatedly proved upon the healthy: Allopathy prescribes her violent drugs in accordance with the traditions which have been handed down from the sorcerers, the alchemists, and the humoral pathologists of old.

Homœopathy recognises only a single law of cure, and upon this law her whole system is founded: Allopathy announces numerous and contradictory laws both of theory and practice, but in her vague, and empirical *routine*, adopts none of them.

Finally, Homœopathy relies solely upon the successful cures she accomplishes, for her prosperity and advancement: Allopathy, with no sound arguments to sustain her, haunted by the ghosts of innumerable victims which she has sent out of the world prematurely, and execrated by thousands of haggard living beings whose constitutions have been ruined by her destructive poisons, relies upon misrepresentations, calumnies, collegiate persecutions, and impotent denunciations, to arrest the progress of her increasingly powerful rival, and to retain the small influence she still maintains over a portion of the lower classes.

After commenting at considerable length upon the wide range of doses employed by the homœopath, and endeavoring to similate the laws which govern the operations of imponderable agents with those which pertain to crude substances, Dr. Hooker arrives at the sage conclusion that "the range of doses in Allopathy is somewhat smaller than the range of doses in homœopathic practice."

We freely concede the truth of this observation, and shall endeavor to adduce some reasons for this difference in "ranges."

We take it for granted that every man of common sense acknowledges the vast powers of imponderable agents, whether of vegetable, animal, or mineral origin. We suppose it will also be conceded, that the laws which govern the actions of these agents, whether operating chemically, morbifically, or medicinally, are as yet entirely unknown, although ample observation has demonstrated that they are as strongly pronounced as those which we observe in the reactions of ponderable substances.

The absurdity and sophistry, therefore, of entering

into arithmetical calculations, and of alluding to differences in weight and bulk, when treating upon imponderable substances of all descriptions, will be apparent to the commonest intellect. We should consider the man an idiot who would be guilty of such folly when writing or speaking of contagious or epidemic substances, malaria, or the molecules of electricity, caloric, and air; and he would certainly be no less foolish who would attempt to bring his arithmetic or his chemistry to bear upon other matters in this kind.

If, then, experience has taught the homœopathist that a wide range of imponderable attenuations may be used with advantage in his various therapeutical measures, what sensible man will have the presumption to gainsay the principle's utility? Because the crude doses of Allopathy, which act mechanically, chemically, or as corrosives, upon the delicate structures of the body, absolutely require to be limited in range, does it follow that the subtile and imponderable doses of Homœopathy should be subjected to similar regulations?

By sad experience, the old school physician finds that he cannot give more than 30 or 40 grains of quinine, daily, for several successive days, without killing his patient. If he prescribes only three or four grains a day, he does not often cure, but establishes a new disease in the liver, which is superadded to that he attempts to cure. The process in this case is analogous to that adopted in France, in stuffing geese, so that their livers may become enlarged sufficiently to make *pâté de foi gras*. His range of doses is thus necessarily limited, for it would be beneath his dignity to use quinine in smaller doses than one grain, and he knows it is pretty certain to kill if he exceeds thirty grains. It would perhaps afford him infinite pleasure if he *could* cram his patient with the entire contents of an apothecary's shop, but when he contemplates such a course, a skeleton flits before him, and he desists.

In his use of calomel, the allopathist allows himself more freedom. In New England, doses as small as one-tenth of a grain are employed, and ten grains are considered a full dose; but at the South and West, calomel is given in doses of sixty and seventy grains, and often repeated, until five and six hundred grains have been taken, or until the patient is destroyed. This is a pretty wide range, considering the nature of the drug; and the discrepancy in the doses of the northern and southern allopathists, is somewhat notable; but the argument of the South is, that these large doses are not so apt to get into the blood as the smaller doses of the North, and that therefore they are less annoyed with those dreadful cases of necroses of the bones, mercurial palsy, rheumatism, nodes, ulceration, gangrene, and sloughing of the gums, mouth, and throat, loss of teeth, mercurial erethism, mercurial dysentery, etc., than are their northern brethren.

The allopathic range then, in the case of calomel, is from one-tenth of a grain to sixty or seventy grains. He cannot descend lower than the sixteenth of a grain, because it would indicate a leaning towards homœopathic doses, which would ill become him; and he cannot advance in the other direction for fear of murdering his patient. Professional expediency on the one hand, and necessity on the other, again govern him.

With respect to other medicines, he is restrained by the same causes. On one side he beholds the small doses of Homœopathy, and his self-conceit, his pride, and his ignorant dislike of everything pertaining to the new system, deter him from making any innovations in this direction. On the other hand, the stringent laws against direct murder and manslaughter, serve to keep him just within certain prescribed bounds.

On page 76, we find this statement: "If both ordinary doses and infinitesimal ones cure disease, they must obviously do it in different ways. The action of the potentized infinitesimal upon the system must be regulated by different principles from those which govern the action of the same article in its crude form."

The absurdity of the assertion will at once be apparent, on the examination of a single substance, as mercury, for example. This mineral in any of its ordinary crude forms, and in ordinary doses, causes salivation, fœtid breath, pains in the bones, etc.; if it becomes diffused through the atmosphere in the form of infinitesimal atoms, and these are taken into the blood through the lungs, the same phenomena as in the first instance present themselves—salivation, fœtid breath, etc.

Drugs, as we have before remarked, never lose their identity or specific modes of operation upon the human tissues. By effecting changes in the forms of drugs, we often develop latent properties, and thus add much to their curative spheres; but during this process they lose nothing of their individuality, or of their specific therapeutical properties. Symptoms, therefore, derived from ordinary doses of crude medicines, are as characteristic of their specific actions upon the organism, as are those produced by infinitesimal doses of the same substances.

It is for this reason that every article in the homœopathic Materia Medica has been repeatedly proved in both its crude and attenuated forms, and doses of almost every variety.

The only attempt at *proof* which Dr. Hooker has made to sustain the last quotation, is as follows: If both a rope, and an invisible filament of one, be supposed to raise a heavy weight, they must do it, according to Dr. Hooker, on different principles; and, *therefore*, crude doses and infinitesimal ones must cure diseases on different principles. This syllogism is about as logical and sensible as the one that, "Man is an animal and a horse is an animal—*therefore* a man is a horse."

The idea of likening the laws which govern the subtile operations of the living body, and the medicines acting upon it under the various circumstances of health and disease, to those which preside over inanimate matter, in lifting a weight with a rope, must have been borrowed from that notable allopathist of the last century, who invented the "powders of bull's tail, man's skull and goat's blood," as sovereign remedies in pleurisy. We are daily expecting another essay from Dr. Hooker denouncing the *vis medicatrix naturæ* as a fallacy and humbug, because he cannot tie it to a heavy weight, and raise it into the air, or "trot it out" and make it *perform* according to his allopathic notions.

Again, at page 79, Dr. Hooker remarks: "*They* (the homœopathists) *as a body wholly neglect the study of Anatomy, Physiology, and Pathology.* These have no place in the science of their therapeutics."

Of course Dr. Hooker *knew*, when he penned this calumny, that he was uttering a very absurd as well as wicked falsehood. On the very pages of most of the homœopathic authorities he professes to have examined, "*Anatomy, Physiology, and Pathology*" are constantly treated of, and are always alluded to as important auxiliaries in elucidating the homœopathic theory and practice. Dr. Hooker *knew* that one of the most eminent homœopathic physicians in Europe, Professor Henderson, *actually occupied the chair of Pathology in the University of Edinburgh, at the time he made this infamous assertion.* In the two homœopathic medical colleges of this country, at Philadelphia and Cleveland, "*Anatomy, Physiology, and Pathology*" are as thoroughly taught and are deemed as important to the student, as they are in allopathic colleges, and portions of the homœopathic journals from which he quotes are devoted to these very subjects; but in the face of all these palpable facts, Dr. Hooker has the assurance to publish such a libel!

In order to put the honesty of Dr. Hooker to the test, we hereby offer to stake $1000, for the benefit of the poor of New York, on the result of an examination of the following proposition. We will designate four, six, or more, if desired, of the very *youngest* homœopathic physicians in New York city, and display the knowledge of any one of them against that of Dr. Hooker, in the above named branches—the examinations to be made, and the verdict to be rendered, by any three competent and impartial scholars. Let us see if the gentleman is as bold in testing *facts* as he is in making this sort of *assertions*. We do not believe that a single homœopathic physician can be found, either in this country or in Europe, who does not esteem a knowledge of Anatomy, Physiology, and Pathology, not merely important, but absolutely essential to a proper appreciation and practice of his profession.

In his pathological investigations, the homœopathist does not indeed place much reliance upon the autopsical appearances presented by those who have died under allopathic treatment, on account of the difficulty of distinguishing between the changes which have arisen from the natural disease, and those which have been caused by the poisonous drugs employed during the treatment. In a majority of the cases of death under allopathic management, it is always a matter of much difficulty to determine whether the *disease*, or the *treatment* of it, has contributed most towards the fatal issue; and it is on this account that the pathology of Allopathy is so defective and unworthy of confidence. But in all cases where individuals have died from natural disease alone, or from poisonous doses of drugs, homœopathists have uniformly placed a high estimate upon pathological investigations.

The few last pages of Chapter IV. are made up of a series of misstatements, and an absurd exhibition of special pleading respecting what are impudently styled the "*inconsistencies*" of homœopathic provings with crude and attenuated medicines, doses, etc.

It is amusing to witness the flippancy with which the writer seeks to pervert the ideas of Hahnemann and his followers, *by inventing his own data*, and then arguing against Homœopathy on the strength of the positions which he falsely attributes to Hahnemann. For example, he everywhere implies that according to the homœopathic doctrine, drugs lose their identity, and become so altered in all respects by the process of attenuation, that entirely new and opposite properties are developed in them, so that their modes of action must be directly the reverse of what they were in the crude state! Thus, at page 89, we find the following: "They (homœopathists) record in their collections of provings, indiscriminately, symptoms occurring under the use of both crude drugs and dynamized infinitesimals; though they assert that the latter act upon the system by virtue of a new power given to them in their preparation, and of course cannot produce effects analogous to those of the former."

To prove the utter mendacity of the last part of this quotation, we copy this statement from page 136 of Hahnemann's Organon: "It is necessary to know the *full extent* of the power by virtue of which each medicine excites disease. In other terms, it is requisite that all the morbid symptoms and changes of the health which their action individually is capable of producing in the economy shall have been observed, as closely as possible, before any one can hope to be able to find or select from among them homœopathic remedies that are appropriate to the greater number of natural diseases."

In no work on Homœopathy has Dr. Hooker ever seen a single observation from which it could be inferred that the effects of crude and attenuated drugs upon the organism, are not analogous. He has everywhere seen, that by the process of attenuation, *latent* properties of drugs become developed, in such a manner that their *entire* specific effects may become manifest upon the human body; but he has never seen it stated that drugs lose their individuality and specific kind of action under any circumstances, or that new and opposite properties are communicated to them by the process of attenuation.

"The entire curative virtues of medicines depend solely upon the power they have of modifying the state of health." (Organon.) It matters not whether this "modification of the state of health" be produced by a large or small dose, or by a crude or attenuated medicine; it is the correspondence of the primitive symptoms caused by the drug, with those of the natural disease, to which the homœopath looks in the selection of his remedy. This is his great therapeutical law, and this his chief guide in the treatment of diseases.

The homœopathic Materia Medica is made up of primitive symptoms, derived from very numerous experiments made by men of undoubted integrity, with both crude and attenuated medicines. In conducting these experiments the utmost regularity, accuracy, and care have always been observed, and those symptoms only retained which have *repeatedly* and *uniformly* been experienced by different experimenters, in different countries, at different periods, and under a great variety of circumstances. Nearly all of these provings have likewise been corroborated by cases of accidental poisonings reported by our opponents, and by pathological facts. What more than this can be reasonably required to substantiate the reality and the perfect accuracy of the facts under consideration.

Throughout the whole of his essay the writer is constantly working himself into a passion, because Hahnemann and his disciples, in carrying out their therapeutical law to its full and legitimate extent, have deemed it proper to make use of medicines of a great variety of strengths, from the mother tinctures up to very high dilutions. In commenting upon this subject, Dr. Hooker involves himself in repeated contradictions; for while he concedes that Hahnemann, in the first instance, practised in accordance with *similia* with ordinary doses of crude medicines, he is constantly pretending that only infinitesimal doses are really homœopathic, and in accordance with the doctrines of Hahnemann. Why did the author of Homœopathy direct the preparation of a variety of strengths of drugs, from the strongest tinctures up to the thirtieth dilutions, and point out examples in which these different preparations should be employed, unless he considered this scale of strengths harmonious with his great law of cure, and of practical utility? Why has he so repeatedly inculcated the importance of selecting remedies of such strengths as shall be most appropriate in each case, in order that the curative reactions may be no more violent than necessary to restore the disordered parts? We reply, for the almost universally conceded reason that the tissues of the human organism, during disease, are subject to a very great variety of degrees of susceptibility to medicinal impressions. Dr. Hooker may affect to despise this self-evident fact, both in theory and practice, and continue to dose his patients indiscriminately, as heretofore, with scruple doses of calomel and jalap, etc., but Heaven help the delicate human structures thus empirically assailed.

Allusion is made at page 90, and in other places, to the employment of "allopathic doses" of tincture of camphor in cholera, by Hahnemann and his followers. This, like most of the other assertions in the book, is simply false. Dr. Hooker *knows* that he cannot point to a single homœopathic writer who has ever advised camphor or any other medicine in "allopathic doses." Tincture of camphor has been prescribed in cholera by homœopathists, in doses of one, and possibly two drops, but never in the usual allopathic doses of fifty or sixty drops. In all the instances, therefore, where he has spoken of the use of "allopathic doses," in disease, by homœopathic physicians, the reader may rest assured that he has published what he knew, while writing it, to be untrue. We are aware that allopathists have been forced, by the great influence of Homœopathy upon the public mind, and by their lack of confidence in their system, to diminish their doses to a very great extent, but this significant fact does not justify the calumny to which we have just referred. Our amiable opponents would doubtless be very glad to restrict Homœopathy, by defining what particular dilution shall be exclusively adopted ; and also to appropriate, as many of them have already attempted to do, our therapeutical law, *similia similibus curantur.* But when future generations shall look back upon the records of those who have made the most important discoveries in medical science, the name of Samuel Hahnemann will stand foremost in the list, while those who now asperse him and his doctrines will be among jests and wonders that are half forgotten.

CHAPTER V.

THE INCONSISTENCIES OF ALLOPATHY AND HER ADVOCATES.

In chapter V. of the "evidences," it is asserted that all cures which take place under homœopathic treatment are attributable to the kindly operations of the *vis medicatrix naturæ*, and that the numerous deaths which occur under allopathic treatment must be placed to the account of "bad Allopathy."

From these luminous "evidences," the reader is left to infer that Homœopathy has only been tested in a "few families," and in a few "chronic cases,"— that its advocates are quacks, fools, liars, artful, dishonest, impudent, altogether destitute of judgment. To support these astounding "evidences" the writer has advanced two most noticeable confirmations, viz.: 1st, his own assertion; and, 2d, a wonderful medicine box which was picked up in New-York many years ago, containing calomel, morphine, tartar emetic, &c., with a number of homœopathic phials containing pellets!

These potent "evidences" are so ably enforced by the constant use of the classical epithets above alluded to, and by such assumptions of wisdom and talent on the part of the author, that a reply seems to be almost out of the question. What can be said, when physicians of such disinterested benevolence, and such utter disregard of their own interests as Dr. Hooker and his "judicious allopathists," choose to constitute themselves judges, and assume to themselves all the talent, all the acquirements, all the honesty, and all the discretion, in medicine, and to denounce all other men and all other systems? Does it not become all the rest of the world—who cannot appreciate facts of a medical nature, who are "loose reasoners," "deluded," etc., etc.,—to bow in humble submission to the imposing dictum, and to the disinterested dictation of these medical oracles?

With respect to the "*box*," it has two sides to it, *one* of which only has been displayed by Dr. Hooker. We shall expose its *other* side. It is a fact which is perfectly well known, that many allopathic practitioners are in the constant habit of using homœopathic medicines by stealth, and of giving the credit of the cures thus made to Allopathy. The sale of homœopathic medicines to allopathic physicians has been for a number of years past a source of no inconsiderable income to the homœopathic pharmacies, and we are credibly informed that this traffic is rapidly increasing. Now, is it strange that these allopathists, who thus secretly employ our remedies, should continue to retain among their newly acquired treasures, a few of their stereotyped drugs, like calomel, morphine, and tartar emetic? The allopath to whom this mysterious "box" probably belonged, might have been floating about in the dusky mazes of eclecticism, delirious, and frightened hither and thither by the delusive phantoms of ancient Allopathy, but yet possessing an instinctive consciousness of the truth of Homœopathy, when he dropped his prize.

We know that it would have been a very easy matter, and quite in character, for some of our unscrupulous opponents to have prepared a box like the one referred to, and to have dropped it, designedly, in order to manufacture from the circumstance "arguments" and "evidences" against our system, but upon the whole, our charity inclines us to adopt the first hypothesis as the most probable one.

On page 100, we find a phenomenon in medical literature, in the form of a *definition of modern Allopathy.* In its line it is remarkably unique, and illustrates most forcibly the definiteness, uniformity, precision, clearness, and beautiful simplicity of the "regular" old-school system. We quote: "But what is Allopathy? Is it one thing—one mode—one system? By no means. This term is applied to all kinds of practice pursued by all regular physicians. It is a very extended, and a very diversified combination. It includes much that is good, and much that is bad. And the practitioners of this Allopathy are, some of them, bad practitioners."

Let us illustrate this subject, as defined by Dr. Hooker. That Allopathy is a mere hotch-potch of vague ideas, of the most diverse and contradictory characters, derived empirically from all sorts of sources, and, as a consequence, possessing nothing definite or certain either in theory or practice, we have for a long time been fully aware; but we confess we were not prepared to see the crumbling skeleton exposed to the gaze of the world by an allopathist. From its extraordinary comprehensiveness, it is eminently worthy of the paternity of the prescription alluded to in another part of this essay, containing 100 different and contradictory ingredients. With such a "very extended and diversified combination of modes of practice," all tastes can surely be suited, from the blood-letting Sangrado, and the heroic dispenser of calomel and opium, to the mincing gum-water expectant, and the scientific prescriber of "powders of bull's tail, boar's tooth, and man's skull," or the "spirit and volatile salt of vipers, and man's blood." Indeed, so "very extensive and diversified" is this "combination which constitutes Allopathy," that within the last few years, the homœopathic law of cure has been added to the list, with many of its principal remedies, and its drop doses! It is true that these men of "very extended and diversified combinations" consider it beneath their propriety to learn the actual nature of homœopathic drugs, and their applicability in disease, but prefer to employ them empirically, as the gambler throws his dice, trusting to "luck and chance" for the result. With these "diversified combinations" allopathists can pander to the fancies of "all kinds of men and the advocates of all kinds of systems."

The attempted introduction of the homœopathic law, with its remedies and doses into Allopathy, affords an excellent illustration of the consistency, honesty, and disinterestedness of the practitioners of the old school. Fifty years ago this doctrine of *similia similibus curantur*, and such medicines as aconite for fevers, belladonna for scarlatina, arnica for mechanical injuries, etc., encountered the ridicule and bitter opposition of the entire body of our opponents, and the very idea of prescribing any of these tinctures in *single drop doses* was scouted as especially absurd and unscientific. But modern Allopathy, with her bony arms extended wide, is attempting to grasp these heresies in her slimy and deadly embrace, like a false fiend of darkness in pursuit of beauty and truth. The genius of knowledge, however, is destined to triumph over the demons of error and bigotry, and truth, in the contest before us, will prevail.

We could cite numerous examples to demonstrate the "very extended, and very diversified combinations" of principles by which different practitioners of the old school are guided in the treatment of disease; but we shall confine ourselves to a brief description of a case of recent occurrence in this city, as a fair sample of the practical operation of the "different modes, systems, and kinds of practice" now so much in vogue with the "regular physicians." We allude to the case of the late J. Kearney Rodgers, M. D.

For the facts in the case, we are indebted to a pamphlet by Alexander E. Hosack, M. D., of New-York, with the following title: "History of the case of the late John Kearney Rodgers, M. D., addressed to the profession." (C. S. Francis & Co., 282 Broadway, New-York.)

According to the records of Dr. Hosack, it appears

that Dr. Rodgers was taken ill on the 9th of October, 1851, with a slight chill, nausea, uneasiness in the right side, and slight pain in the bowels.

On Saturday, the 11th, Dr. Dubois called in and prescribed a Seidlitz powder.

On Sunday, the 12th, Dr. Wilkes was consulted, and, regarding the disease "functional disorder of the liver," administered two pills of blue mass, to be followed by a Seidlitz powder.

On the 13th and 14th, Dr. Hosack attended and found him free from fever, with a white, slightly coated tongue with a dingy hue at the base, pain in the bowels, slight uneasiness in the hypochondriac region, full and slightly accelerated, compressible pulse. "Regarding these symptoms as indicative of a *biliary congestion*," Dr. H. advised an emetic or ten grains of calomel, which, however, were declined by the patient. On the evening of this day Dr. Dubois was called in consultation with Dr. Hosack, and pronounced the symptoms "*bilious remittent fever*."

On Wednesday, the 15th, these two "regular" gentlemen again met in consultation, one of them naming the symptoms "congestion of the liver," and the other calling them "bilious remittent fever." Here we have a commencement of the "extended and diversified combination" of practical Allopathy.

Dr. Delafield was added to the consultation on Friday evening, Oct. 17th, and declaring the disease to be "bilious remittent fever," advised a discontinuance of the mercurial pills which had been prescribed by Dr. Hosack on the 15th, and a substitution of the "usual febrifuge medicines." Here again we have a beautiful practical illustration of the "diversified combination" system of Allopathy. According to one gentleman's "system" or "mode" of practice, the patient had a liver complaint, and required calomel: according to the system of the other gentleman, the patient was affected with "bilious remittent fever," and required the "usual febrifuge medicines." If still another "regular" had been added to the consultation he would also have taken advantage of the "very extended and very diversified combination of systems which constitute Allopathy," and named the symptoms typhoid fever, for which opium and bark would have been appropriate. Another, who had made diseases of the kidneys a speciality would have termed it nephritis, and prescribed bleeding, leeching, nitrate of potash, &c. Another, from his veneration of his illustrions predecessors, might have attributed the symptoms to a "derangement of the humors," and ordered "powders of bull's tail, crab's eyes, and goat's blood, or volatile spirit and salt of vipers, and man's blood." Another, if he had recently returned from Paris, would have called the malady a gastro-enteritе, and insisted on the leeching and gum-water "mode."

These are only a few of the "very diversified combinations" which might be adduced to illustrate the certainty and precision of Allopathy. As we advance with the case under consideration it will be observed that Homœopathy has not escaped, but has been mixed up in admirable confusion with the "combination."

From the 17th to the 22d of October the symptoms were about as follows: "General restlessness, imperfect sleep, depression of spirits, anxious countenance, slight fever, increased sallowness, accelerated pulse, and at times moderate perspiration." During this entire period the "usual febrifuge medicines" were employed, and it was not until frequent rigors set in, followed by profuse perspirations, that this "kind of practice" was abandoned and "another mode" adopted, consisting of "quinine in ten and five grain doses, at intervals of several hours, *which was continued for several successive days.* The positive effect of quinine was in due time made manifest by *ringing in the ears* and almost *total deafness!*"

The "very extended, and very diversified combination" practice stands out again most prominently. But why the attention of these gentlemen should have been directed to the ears of their patient, we cannot imagine. Why the auditory structures should be treated to cure a "bilious fever," must puzzle all but such "close reasoning" prodigies, as the author of the "Evidences."

According to Dr. Delafield, however, this particular "combination," or "mode," or "system," was productive of no benefit, as the patient continued to get worse. And the learned doctor now ascertained "that there was something in the case that he could not understand!" There was no difficulty in understanding the "*ringing in the ears*," and the "almost *total deafness*," and if the gentleman had consulted a homœopathic Materia Medica, and examined the proving of quinine, he would have had no difficulty in comprehending most of the other symptoms of the case. Were an individual to administer to a stout mastiff, ten grains of quinine every few hours, for six days in succession, and the act could be proved against him, he would be indicted and punished for wanton cruelty to animals. But dog doctors are not "regular," they have no "very extended and very diversified combinations," and they cannot trace their origin beyond the dark ages—therefore, dog and horse doctors should be held responsible for their poisonings.

At this stage of the case, it was deemed expedient to try a new "mode," a new "system," a new "combination," and accordingly, "tincture of *aconite* was prescribed in doses of *one drop* each," in alternation with large doses of aromatic sulphuric acid. The acid was given for the avowed "purpose of arresting the excessive sweats," but no reason was ascribed for the employment of homœopathic doses of a homœopathic remedy. The legitimate inference, therefore, is, that aconite was brought into requisition on account of its general use in fevers, by homœopathic practitioners. This must be true, because, in no allopathic work is this medicine advised as a remedy in "bilious remittent," or other fever. We are aware that this is only carrying out the "diversified combinations" so *naïvely* described by Dr. Hooker in his definition of Allopathy, and it is probable that the remedy would have proved successful, if the disease had really been a "bilious remittent fever." But in justice to Homœopathy, we are compelled to declare, that there was not a single symptom from the commencement to the termination of the case of Dr. Rodgers, for which aconite was indicated, therefore its inefficiency, and the propriety of ranking it with the empirical remedies which were so freely employed in the case. Respecting the allopathic dose of tincture of aconite, their most reputable pharmacopœias place it at fifteen drops, to be gradually increased as circumstances require. We leave the reader to draw his own inference in the matter.

October 24th, 25th, 26th, 27th, and 28th, passed by without any amendment of the symptoms, the patient having taken, during this period, occasional doses of quinine and purgative pills.

The drop doses of aconite were resumed again on the 29th, and continued, with elixir vitriol, quinine, laudanum, nitro-muriatic acid, and effervescent draughts, up to November 5, when the aconite was discontinued, and the unfortunate gentleman gradually sunk into death under the use of quinine, laudanum, and brandy and water.

According to Dr. Hosack's "system" of Allopathy, the malady was a liver complaint, for which emetics and calomel were the specific remedies; and this physician is quite satisfied, that if his mode of practice had been pursued, the patient would have *recovered.* According to the Allopathy of Dr. Delafield, the disease was "bilious remittent fever," for the cure of which a "very extended, and very diversified combination" of remedies was necessary, like febrifuge medicines and quinine in ten grain doses; aromatic sulphuric acid in large doses, and tincture of aconite in single drop doses; cathartic pills and laudanum in teaspoonful doses; effervescent draughts and elixir of vitriol.

What particular "system" or "combination" of Allopathy the other medical gentlemen would have adopted if they had been allowed to exercise their own unprompted judgments in the case, we cannot imagine, but there is every reason to suppose that they would not have confined themselves to "one thing—one mode—one system," but that "all kinds of practice," and the most "diversified combinations" would have been called into requisition.

It may be urged that homœopathic physicians might also have mistaken this case, and we concede the validity of the argument, if it is merely intended to apply to the classification of the symptoms under some particular name. But the homœopathist never prescribes for groups of symptoms as a unit. He never regards the name which may be given to a disease, in the selection of his remedy, but each individual phenomenon connected with the case commands his special attention, and is taken into consideration in making up his prescription. It is in no degree of consequence to him whether the disease is designated by this or that name; he looks only at symptoms, and endeavors to combat them as they arise, by appropriate medicines.

Not so, however, with the allopathist. His venerated medical fathers have taught him that every malady and every group of symptoms must have some particular name, and that his remedial measures must be directed with reference to this name, and not to symptoms. His first care, therefore, is to ascertain what especial appellation best fits his case, and then to search his authorities for the appropriate remedies. Should the symptoms not be fully developed, and he gives them a wrong name, as is so often the case, the most fearful practical results often ensue.

Dr. Hooker speaks of "good Allopathy" and "bad Allopathy," of "judicious allopathists and injudicious allopathists." Now as this gentleman has constituted himself judge and arbiter of everything pertaining to medical science, will he inform the world who, of all the eminent physicians who attended Dr. Rodgers, were judicious and who injudicious, and which of the "modes" suggested was "bad Allopathy" and which "good Allopathy"? As human life is of some consequence, and as Allopathy consists of so many different "things, modes, systems, combinations, and kinds of practice," and as eminent physicians constantly differ so widely in the diagnosis and treatment of disease, will the medical dictator point out some way of distinguishing "judicious Allopathy" from "bad Allopathy?" Will he tell us in what cases "powders of bull's tail, and volatile salt of vipers" should be given —when drop doses of tincture of aconite should be prescribed—when the gums, mouth and throat should be made to mortify and slough from mercury—when "ringing in the ears and almost total deafness" should be produced by quinine—in what stage of bilious fever laudanum should be administered in teaspoonful doses—whether opium and brandy, or venesection, calomel and antimony, should be relied on in typhus fevers—whether single drop doses of the tinctures of camphor, aconite, etc., in cholera and fevers, are allopathic or homœopathic; and if the former, from what old school authority, besides the "evidences" of Dr. Hooker, are these minute doses derived—whether bleeding and calomel, so boldly employed by some old school gentlemen in cholera, do really kill or cure patients; or whether opium, or rhubarb, or astringents, or gum-water, or the ethers, or brandy, or Hahnemann's specific, camphor, in drop doses, all of which are used by different practitioners, should be employed in this fearful malady—when shall we prescribe according to the *contraria contrariis opponenda*, when according to *similia similibus curantur*, when according to the *antipathic*, or the *expectant*, or the *Brumorian*, or any of the other "diversified combinations" which go to make up Allopathy. Will Dr. Hooker have the kindness to put himself into a pair of very high-heeled boots with red tops, mount the town-pump of Norwich, Connecticut, inflate his cheeks to the fullest capacity, and announce to our deluded human nature, who, beside himself, can distinguish "judicious Allopathy" from "bad Allopathy"? After accomplishing this duty, will he be pleased to set his arms akimbo, advance one foot forward, *à la Napoleon*, and issue another decision declaring who, in addition to his modest self, may be considered "practitioners of a judicious Allopathy?" These requests are made for the benefit of allopathists alone, for the decree has already gone forth respecting those homœopathists who have been converted from Allopathy. We, deluded converts, of course bow in abject submission before the majesty of genius—the extraordinary judgment, the vast knowledge, the wonderful "mathematical powers," the "close reasoning," the "very extended, and very diversified combinations," the honesty, integrity, disinterestedness, charity, morality and piety which pertain to Dr. Hooker, *et id omne genus*. His peculiar acumen and "close reasoning" have taught him that such men as Henderson, Joslin, Tessier, Croserio, Roth, Teste, Dudgeon, Drysdale, Laurie, Russel, Currie, Rose, Gross, Stapff, Fleischmann, Rapou, Molin, Madden, Scott, Quinn, Simon, Black, Bayard, Gray, Metcalf, Cox, Kitchen, and the many thousand other converts from the "diversified combinations which constitute Allopathy," are all either knaves and fools, or actuated by "pecuniary considerations!" How unfortunate that these deluded and unhappy gentlemen had not been blessed with a moiety of the penetration, the profound sense, the honesty, and the disinterestedness of Dr. Hooker! How unfortunate that this brilliant sun of Norwich did not shine at the commencement, instead of the middle of the nineteenth century, so that the petty labors of such an intelligence as that of Samuel Hahnemann might have been annihilated in the beginning!

It is by no means a pleasing task to wade through the mass of silly fallacies, and mean misrepresentations which everywhere pervade Dr. Hooker's labored essay, and we shall not therefore weary the reader by noticing all of his unfair assertions, and his impotent denunciations of Homœopathy and its advocates. It would be an easy thing to prove nearly the whole publication, page by page, a tissue of flimsy sophistries respecting the homœopathic system, and of unfounded accusations against its advocates, but they are so palpable and absurd in their character, and the vindictiveness, envy, and spite of their author are so apparent, that such a course is not necessary. We shall therefore only allude particularly in our remaining paragraphs to a few of those "towering" statements, upon which considerable stress is laid.

Several pages of the present chapter are devoted to Dr. Hooker's own assertions respecting the incompetency of homœopathic physicians, or of laymen, to judge of facts in medical science, and it is most earnestly advised that the people who had the profoundest interest in the subject should rely solely upon the superior wisdom, keen penetration, and *peculiar* tact of such "close reasoning" philanthropists as himself. He informs his readers that the statistics of homœopathic practice are of no account, because homœopathic families have scarcely any *acute* diseases, but such as are, for the most part, either *chronic* or imaginary; or if, by chance, a grave disorder should happen to exist, that an allopathic physician is instantly sent for! A reply to such an absurd assertion as this would of course be superfluous.

But in alluding to statistics, the writer very studiously avoids all mention of the homœopathic hospitals of Europe, several of which have for many years been open to all observers. We shall in some measure supply this omission by the following brief quotation from Professor Henderson's reply to Professor Simpson's pamphlet on Homœopathy:

"Dr. Fleischmann, of the homœopathic hospital of Vienna, at various periods, has published the results of his treatment of inflammation of the lungs between the years 1834 and 1848—the latter being the last period for which his statistics have reached me. Dr. Reiss, of the homœopathic hospital at Lintz, Dr. Schweitzer, of the homœopathic hospital at Kremsier, and Dr. Tessier, of the hospital of Sainte-Marguerite of Paris, also have published the statistics of their homœopathic treatment of the same disease, and the collective results are as follows:—728 cases of inflammation of the lungs, 35 deaths, or one death in 21 cases; less than five per cent. In my letter to Dr. Forbes, I have given an account of the comparative success, in the same disease, of the best hospital physicians, who use allopathic remedies, in Paris; they furnish 531 cases, of which 81 died, or one in six and two-thirds, or about fifteen per cent. In the 'Introduction to the Study of Homœopathy' (to which, and to the letter to Dr. Forbes, the reader is referred for a more detailed discussion of this most important subject) various allopathic authorities are referred to as furnishing 909 cases of this disease, with 212 deaths, or 23.32 per cent.; nearly one death in every four cases. In the same work is contrasted the mortality under each system of treatment, in pleurisy and peritonitis, and the same vast superiority of the homœopathic practice is exhibited—the mortality of the former disease having been in Fleischmann's practice, among 224 cases, only one in 72, and of the latter, among 105 cases, one in 21; while under the ordinary system, the mortality was from 8 to 16 times greater. The absence of sufficiently large statistics on the allopathic side, renders these last comparisons less satisfactory than in the instance of inflammation of the lungs; and in regard to other acute inflammations, we have no data whatever from Allopathy to enable us to form an estimate of its inferiority. I may add, however, that besides the diseases mentioned above, Dr. Fleischmann's table for the eight years prior to 1844, shows 181 cases of erysipelas of the face, and only two deaths; 31 cases of inflammation of the membranes of the heart, without a single death; 44 cases of dysentery, and two deaths;—results which are far beyond the reach of any other known method of treatment." *

"Dr. Forbes, apparently surprised at the results published in one of Dr. Fleischmann's tables, yet combatting the notion that the cases must have been slight which recovered under what are commonly believed inadequate means, observes, 'It would be very unreasonable to believe that, out of 300 cases of pneumonia (inflammation of the lungs), 224 cases of pleurisy, and 105 of peritonitis (in all 629 cases), spread over a period of eight years, *all* the cases, except the fatal cases (27 in number), were slight, and such as would have seemed to us hardly requiring treatment of any kind. In fact, according to all experience, such could not be the case. But independently of this *a priori* argument, we have sufficient evidence to prove that many of the cases of pneumonia, at least, were severe cases. A few of these cases are reported in detail by Dr. Fleischmann himself, and we have ourselves had the statement corroborated by the private testimony of a physician (not a homœopath) who attended Dr. Fleisch-

* "Since 1844, the German hospital statistics give us 164 cases of erysipelas, without a death; 84 of peritonitis, with 4 deaths; 75 of pleurisy with one death."

mann's ward for three months.' * And he says of Dr. Fleischmann, that he 'is a regular, well-educated physician, as capable of forming a true diagnosis as other practitioners, and he is considered by those who know him as a man of honor and respectability, and incapable of attesting a falsehood.' Of the whole 728 cases to which I have alluded above, 616 occurred in the hospital of this trustworthy observer. From my own experience in the treatment of inflammation of the lungs, and other acute diseases,† I have not a doubt of the thorough accuracy of the accounts given us by the physicians to whom I have referred. But how do allopathic physicians get rid of these remarkable statements? Some by denying their truth (for there are men who will deny anything), and some, Dr. Forbes among them, by ascribing all to the bountiful hand of Unassisted Nature! If this latter view of the subject be the correct one, then it is obvious that the medical men who believe it to be so should cease from all medical treatment in acute diseases. That it is not, however, the correct view of the matter, appears very clearly from the cases published by M.

* "Brit. and For. Med. Rev., p. 243, No. 41."

† "I have treated homœopathically throughout 16 cases of pneumonia, with one death: 10 cases of croup, without a death; besides a few cases of pericarditis, pleurisy, peritonitis, and many of dysentery, bronchitis, and erysipelas, with only two deaths, one from dysentery in an old man long in bad health, the other from general bronchitis in an infant. In one case only was blood-letting adopted. Of other acute diseases, I have treated homœopathically 39 of measles, without a death; 45 of hooping-cough, with one death; and 36 of scarlet fever, with two deaths. Among the last 2 deaths, one is included of a gentleman who, having recovered from the fever, was seized with inflammation of the chest, and was treated during the greater part of that, his last illness, by Dr. Alison."

Grisolle. He left eleven *mild* cases of inflammation of the lungs to follow their natural course,* and we find that the consequences of the disease were not gone in any till the end of the third, and in some not till the end of the fourth week, whereas, under the homœopathic treatment, every trace of the disease is usually gone, in severe cases too, in a third of that time,† proving that Homœopathy is not a merely passive system."

With regard to the great number of cases here adduced in illustration of the vast superiority of homœopathic treatment in the diseases under consideration, let it be observed that nearly all of them occurred in public hospitals which have always been open to the inspection of physicians of every school; that the symptoms and treatment of each case were minutely recorded from day to day; that these records were constantly open to the investigation of all who chose to examine them; and that critical investigation has always been solicited by the physicians of these hospitals. In view of these circumstances, and of the incontrovertible fact that a majority of these cases were treated under the immediate observation of allopathic physicians, who have vouched for their accuracy and fairness, it is evident that none but the most ungenerous and uncandid would ever presume to deny their entire correctness, or to decry the reputations of the distinguished gentlemen who have charge of these institutions.

Throughout the whole of his unscrupulous tirade

* "See Letter to Dr. Forbes."

† "See for ample details, 'Recherches Cliniques,' par J. P. Tessier, Paris, 1850."

against Homœopathy, Dr. Hooker has constantly evinced the quality of his spirit, by imputing a lack of fairness, lack of talent, lack of education, lack of social position, and lack of responsibleness, to homœopathic physicians. He has evidently no personal knowledge of a single member of our profession, nor has he any data on which to form an opinion respecting the abilities or integrity of its advocates, yet like the cornered reptile, he bites at everything within his reach.

With regard to this subject, we take the occasion to inform Dr. Hooker and his coadjutors that men of real knowledge, and talent, and who firmly believe in the truth of doctrines they profess, are never obliged to misrepresent the opinions, or to write falsely of the characters of those who differ from them. Such a course is not only an indication of intellectual weakness and vindictiveness, but it goes far to prove inherent defects in views they advocate. Those who are confident in the soundness of their doctrines, and actually possess knowledge, and critical sagacity, are not apt to assume to themselves these qualifications, and constitute themselves judges of others, but they prefer that those who are disinterested should decide in the matter.

That the public may not be misled by the false assertions of our opponents, we deem it proper to declare, that no man is recognised as a homœopathic physician who has not received a thorough medical education in some legally authorised institution, and is in possession of a proper diploma constituting him a doctor of medicine. We have had much intercourse, both as an allopathic and as a homœopathic practitioner, with the members of both schools; and so far as our observation has extended, the practitioners of the new school compare favorably, in all respects to say the least, with those of the old school. In the present condition of Homœopathy, with its vast array of intelligent and discriminating supporters, it appears almost superfluous to refute these malicious imputations of a certain class of our enemies, but as falsehood often repeated, and uncontradicted, may sometimes pass as truth, we have alluded to the subject, and take the liberty of subjoining the opinion of a liberal and enlightened opponent, the distinguished Dr. Forbes, formerly editor of the British and Foreign Medical Review, as an offset to the uncalled for and unsubstantiated denunciations of the gentleman from Norwich, Connecticut.

"No doctrine, however ingenious, not based on positive demonstrable facts, will any more be regarded but as a piece of poetical speculation, which may indeed amuse the fancy, but can never influence the conduct of scientific men, much less of practical physicians. But Homœopathy comes before us in a much more imposing aspect, and claims our attention on grounds which cannot be gainsayed. It presents itself as a new art of medicine, as a mode of practice utterly at variance with that long established in the world; and claims the notice of mankind on the irresistible ground of its superior power of curing diseases and preserving human life. And it comes before us now, not in the garb of a suppliant, unknown and helpless, but as a conqueror, powerful, famous, and triumphant. The disciples of Hahnemann are spread over the whole civilized world. There is not a town of any considerable size in Germany, France, Italy, England or America, that does not boast of possessing one or more homœopathic physicians, not a few of whom are men of high respectability and learning; many of them in large practice, and patronized especially by persons of high rank. New books on Homœopathy issue in abundance from the press; and journals, exclusively devoted to its cause, are printed and widely circulated in Europe and America. Numerous hospitals and dispensaries for the treatment of the poor, on the new system, have been established, many of which publish reports blazoning its successes, not merely in warm phrases, but in the hard words, and harder figures of statistical tables."

On the last pages of this chapter we find a repetition of an old *ex parte* statement, made some fifteen or twenty years ago, by M. Andral of Paris, (a bitter opponent of Homœopathy,) respecting a trial which he made with homœopathic medicines, in one of the Parisian hospitals.

That M. Andral was entirely ignorant of the doctrines of Hahnemann, and of the pathogeneses of the drugs he made use of in this pretended trial, is clearly evident from his own description of the experiment. This fact was conclusively proved at the time, and no one in Paris believed for an instant, that Andral possessed either the knowledge to employ homœopathic remedies properly, or the moral honesty to administer them fairly if he had possessed this knowledge. We suspect that Andral's Homœopathy was very much like that of Drs. Delafield & Co., in the case of the late Dr. Rodgers, when they prescribed "aconite in single drop doses," in alternation with "large doses of aromatic sulphuric acid." We suggest to M. Andral and his admirers the study of the following fable:

"Once upon a time," says Æsop, "a man and a lion were journeying together, and came at length to high words as to which was the braver and stronger creature of the two. As the dispute waxed warmer they happened to pass by, on the road-side, a statue of a man strangling a lion. "See there," said the man, "what more undeniable proof can you have of our superiority than that?" "That," said the lion, "is your version of the story; let us be sculptors, and for one lion under the feet of a man, you shall have twenty men under the paws of the lion."

If M. Andral had invited a competent homœopathic physician to prescribe for the cases to which he alludes, the results would have been marked, and satisfactory; but it was more agreeable to his interests and to his preconceived notions that the experiment should fail, and he therefore selected himself as physician, and prescribed a few homœopathic medicines in an *allopathic* manner, viz.: by the "diversified combination" system of random guesses respecting their applicability in each case.

The practice of Homœopathy does not consist of a vague and indefinite system of "guessing," which can be intuitively adopted by the allopathic followers of routine, without study; but it is a system founded exclusively upon facts, and therefore requires a long course of observance, and the most patient and accurate investigation, in order to apply its therapeutical resources properly. Whenever Andral, or any other allopathic physician, chooses to *learn* the doctrines taught by Hahnemann, and then to employ his specifics honestly and fairly, he will have no reason to doubt the truth of the former, or the great curative powers of the latter.

CHAPTER VI.

HOMŒOPATHY AND ALLOPATHY CONTRASTED.

In this chapter Dr. Hooker professes to give his readers an "estimate of Hahnemann." Before making up this curious "estimate," the writer must have dosed himself largely with some of the "accumulated facts" of Allopathy, in the form of "volatile spirit and volatile salt of vipers," for we do not believe there can be found, in the entire annals of medicine, a more offensive and pitiable exhibition of vindictiveness, or more utter disregard of the common decencies of life, than are here presented. The only "arguments" or "evidences" which are adduced in this mendacious chapter to illustrate the character and labors of Hahnemann, are derived from the morbid imagination of the writer himself, and are such as: "cheat," "medical fanatic," "wild dreamer in science," "absurd theorizer," "scientific fool," "flimsy reasoner," "prone to delusion," "quack," "mongrel," "fantastic," "radical," "fanatic," etc. These are the "arguments," the "evidences," and the "close reasonings," indulged by our opponents; this is the kind of logic employed by modern allopathists to injure a rival method. We have no means of knowing whether this Hippocratic oracle "made up faces," or "tore his hair" while giving expression to these stupendous "evidences," but we have no doubt that he required several of the "powders of bull's tail and man's blood," so highly commended by the great modern light of his school, Dr. Sydenham, in his "*Processus Integri*," before his equilibrium was restored.

But seriously, who can imagine a more disgusting, and yet ludicrous spectacle, than is presented by an individual of such limited capacities, and such palpable dishonesty as the author of the "Evidences, etc.," endeavoring to injure the character of Samuel Hahnemann! On the one hand we have an intellectual giant, whose vast general erudition, profound knowledge of medical science, skill in logic, and laborious personal researches in regard to the nature of drugs, have elicited the highest admiration and respect from every able and honorable allopathist who has ever written respecting him: on the other hand, we have an impotent medical charlatan, who has wasted some fifty pages in efforts to "figure up" the weight of a class of *imponderable* substances, and about as many more in calling hard names, and making up mouths at Homœopathy! The scene reminds us of a Tom Thumb challenging Lord Bacon to intellectual controversy, or of any ridiculous display of weakness against power.

For a period of more than fifty years, Hahnemann devoted his entire energies, mental and physical, to the advancement of medical science. With a mind amply stored with the medical literature of past and contemporary times, reasoning powers of the highest order, and a benevolence and devotion towards his fellow men, unparalleled in the history of any science, he entered upon his glorious mission. At this period, there were no fixed and generally received ideas upon medical topics, but everything was vague, indefinite, and unsatisfactory. Opinions that were deemed orthodox in one country, were denounced as erroneous in another. Hence arose a great variety of modes of practice, of the most contradictory characters, each sustained by its array of strenuous advocacy, but all of them founded upon conjecture, or derived from the absurd dogmas of antiquity.

And this was no new state of things, for the whole history of Allopathy had thus far consisted of nothing but a continued succession of changes in theory and practice. Each generation had continued to advance new ideas respecting the nature and treatment of diseases, and to look back with pity or contempt upon the ages which had gone before.

With all those changes, however, the mortality of the sick had not at all diminished. Patients continued to sicken, to be drugged, and to die, as before, whether under the antiphlogistic, the expectant, the Brunonian, or other mode of treatment. The medical world had so long regarded the doctrines of the ancients with veneration, that nearly all the practical results of these doctrines were retained, although the theoretical parts were rejected as absurd. Let it ever be impressed upon the mind, that blood-letting, emetics, purgatives, sudorifics, etc., originated legitimately and naturally from the "humoral pathology."

Hippocrates announced that the existence of the four humors, viz.: the blood, the phlegm, the yellow bile, and the black bile, in proper proportions in respect to "quantity, quality, and mixture," constituted the healthy condition; and that any variation in the quality or in the proportions of these humors, occasions disease.

His treatment consisted in expelling from the body by bleeding, purging, sweating, etc., a certain amount of any humor which might exist in excessive quantity, and thus restore those proportions which constitute health. If the theoretical opinions of Hippocrates had been correct, if those humors had been actually destined to play the part in the organism which was attributed to them, and if the true cause of disease had consisted in an excess of one or more of them, then the evacuation and correction of these deranged fluids would have been a reasonable, and, perhaps, successful mode of practice.

For many centuries the humoral pathology prevailed almost universally, and the treatment which had been legitimately deduced from this pathology was of course recognised as the chief means of cure. But when totally new ideas obtained theoretically, and the humoral doctrines of the ancients were discarded as fanciful and absurd, it was reasonable to suppose that new theories of cure and new systems of practice would be adopted; but strange as it may be deemed, such was not the fact.

Fifty years ago, the medical world was divided into numerous sects, such as the vitalists, the solidists, the eclectics, the Brunonians, the expectants, etc., each of which entertained peculiar views in regard to the causes and nature of disease; but singular enough, in their practical deductions, all harmonious—all according to the method inculcated by Hippocrates and his heathen cotemporaries, 2000 years before! One attributed disease to a derangement of the "vital properties" of the parts affected, but still persisted in punishing the stomach, bowels, and skin, with emetics, drastics, and sweats! Another ascribed disease to disorder in the solids, but still prescribed the same treatment! Still another recognised only two classes of diseases, the sthenic and asthenic, and yet the same general remedies were adopted! Others still were floating about, entirely undecided in their opinions, but none the less intent on doctoring the poor stomach, bowels, and skin, for the ills of the whole body!

In the midst of such an array of discordant opinions, and such a confused mixture of modern hypotheses with ancient dogmas, the founder of Homœopathy discovered his theory of cure, *similia similibus curantur.* Perceiving at a glance that the errors of those who had preceded him had arisen from too much theorizing, and too great a proneness to substitute hypotheses for facts, he resolved at the onset to rely solely upon facts to substantiate or disprove the idea he had conceived. With this view he originated the proving of drugs upon healthy persons, in order that their specific effects might be fully investigated, and that a foundation might thus be laid for a scientific and rational system of practice. And he most nobly and faithfully carried out his conception—not by drawing upon his imagination, as preceding writers had done—not by referring to the accumulated absurdities of antiquity—not by assuming data on insufficient grounds

—but by a long series of painful and hazardous experiments with drugs in different forms and different doses, *upon his own person.* During the course of these experiments, Hahnemann was not unfrequently made seriously ill for weeks together, often noting with feverish brow and trembling hand, each painful symptom as it occurred.

When examining, a few years since, at Paris, the original provings of Hahnemann, in his own handwriting, we were filled with astonishment and veneration, at the contemplation of the immense labor, disease, and pain, which all these provings must have cost their author, and of the active benevolence which must have prompted them. While tracing the different kinds of writing, here bold and plain, there timid and tremulous, now irregular, and in some cases nearly illegible, we could almost fancy this benefactor of his race in the midst of his trials and his sufferings. When remonstrances were offered by his wife and friends, against the risks to which he continually exposed himself in his experiments, his noble reply was, "What is the comfort or happiness of one man, in comparison with the future welfare of thousands and perhaps millions? or what the life of a single individual, compared to the well-being of generations of men?"

No one ever knew Hahnemann, but to love his personal traits, to admire his brilliant genius and talents, and to revere the benevolent impulses which inspired all his vast efforts in behalf of medical science. Even his strongest opponents, (we mean those who have any pretensions to ability, or are recognized as gentlemen,) have always awarded him a high meed of praise for honesty, genius, talents, and unwearied industry in the investigation of facts. While respectfully differing with him in opinion, they have freely acknowledged his integrity, his profound learning, and his disinterested benevolence.

So far as relates to the great homœopathic law of cure, and to the practice of medicine founded upon it, no "theorizing" ever has been, or ever can be indulged in. It is a law which was logically deduced from absolute facts connected with specific effects of drugs, and which has since been firmly established in science by facts alone. It is not a time-serving law, it admits of no amalgamation with any other hypothesis, "system," "mode," or "combination of practice,"—it recognizes no preconceived or hypothetical data, but it must stand or fall on demonstrated truths. If Homœopathy is true, Allopathy must be false, and *vice versâ*.

Some of our opponents have inquired why Hahnemann and his disciples have not sought to amalgamate their doctrines with those of Allopathy, as Brown, Broussais and others have done? We reply, for the same reason that the Christian religion should not be amalgamated with Mohammedanism, or truth with error.

"Homœopathy," says Dr. Hooker, "has been fairly before medical men for fifty years; and the profession has passed its verdict upon it in the most deliberate and positive manner. Some are disposed to think that this verdict is good for nothing, and openly charge medical men, as a body, with a wilful blindness to the truth of Homœopathy. If this charge be well founded, the medical profession are governed in relation to this doctrine by a spirit altogether different from that which they have manifested towards all other new doctrines and opinions. Look over the whole history of medicine, and observe the course which the profession have pursued, in regard to the numberless doctrines and theories which have arisen from time to time. As they have passed away one after another, they have been examined and sifted by medical men, and while much has been rejected, much has been retained and added to the permanent treasures of our science." (p. 128.)

We do not remember ever to have witnessed a more supremely ridiculous delivery, than this of Dr. Hooker, respecting the "verdicts of allopathic medical men." If any one will take the trouble to "look over the whole history of medicine, and observe the course which the profession have pursued, in regard to the numberless doctrines and theories which have arisen from time to time," the pitiable absurdity of Dr. Hooker's reasoning upon this subject, will be apparent.

Some twenty-two hundred years ago, a doctrine was announced, that the human body contained four different humors. Health was supposed to obtain, when these fluids were all right with respect to "quantity, quality, and mixture;" while diseases were supposed to be produced by any alterations in the proportions or quality of these humors. Upon this hypothesis, a treatment was adopted, as we have already intimated, for the purpose of "purging off" and "correcting" these disordered fluids. The doctrine has been recognised under the name of "*humoral pathology*."

This doctrine was "fairly before medical men," not for fifty years only, but for *two thousand years*, and that too after "the profession had passed its verdict upon it in the most deliberate and positive manner!" That "verdict" was favorable. What a grand illustration of the judgment, the wisdom, the critical acumen, and the profound sagacity of allopathic physicians! What a commentary upon the competency of such "medical men," to decide respecting the merits of a system of medicine! In this instance, the "sifting" process was not even commenced until the families of mankind had been poisoned for more than twenty centuries by such profound and "close reasoning analyzers" as Dr. Hooker and his amiable colaborateurs. The curative efforts of these wise fathers of Allopathy during this long period, were directed to the correction of four imaginary humors. Occasionally, while these centuries were rolling on, an individual would dare to think for himself, and to express an original idea; but instantly the whole "faculty" would frown upon him as an innovator, a disregarder of the "accumulated facts" of antiquity, a man of "loose analogies," a "dreamer in science," and a "quack;" and he would be crushed under the force of a close banded interest. It is true, that a small number, including Themison, Celsus, and Paracelsus, succeeded in attracting the attention of medical men temporarily to their innovations, but the "verdict" for the "humoral pathology and practice" remained fixed and unchangeable until the seventeenth century, when Baglivi originated the doctrine that all morbid changes commenced in the *solids*, and that the fluids were only acted upon secondarily.

Cotemporary with Baglivi was Hoffmann, who adopted the views of the former, but attempted to explain the nature of diseased action by the operation of what he termed spasm or atomy.

From this period until the present time, several medical theories have been introduced, allopathic "medical men" have examined them, and the "verdict" has been in favor of adopting them all in theory, but to abide by no one of them in practice. It is for this reason that the medical world, at the present time, is divided into so many different sects, and that the treatment of disease corresponds to the peculiar pathological notions which each individual physician happens to entertain. No two colleges of medicine teach the same doctrines—no two professors entertain the same theoretical opinions—and as Dr. Hooker well observes, "no one thing, no one mode, no one system, no one kind of practice," generally obtains; but the term Allopathy is applied to a "very extended, and very diversified combination" of contradictory modes of both practice and theory. A graduate of one institution bleeds on all occasions; his "regular" brother, who has received his "bundle of ideas" from another school, denounces blood-letting as pernicious, and commends the almost universal employment of calomel and opium; another university sends forth its students with the impression that most of the ills of humanity are dependent on *gastro-enterite*, and the practical "verdict" is, leeches, and gum-water; and the "verdict" of another college may be in favor of the excitement and collapse, or the sthenic and asthenic theories, and direct its students to beware of any "very diversified combinations" in their practice, but to confine their treatment to stimulation and exhaustion.

Other schools lecture about all theories, believing in no one of them; but as their perplexed pupils must have some method of treating disease, they render their "deliberate and positive verdict" in favor of the bleeding, vomiting, purging, sweating, and blistering system, which was derived from the exploded humoral pathology. Whether any of these schools include among their remedies, the "volatile spirit and salt of vipers," or the "powders of bull's tail, bore's tooth, crab's eyes, and man's blood," we are not informed; but we find these remedies most highly recommended in the treatment of pleurisy, and other maladies, by one of the most eminent of modern allopathists, Sydenham, the "English Hippocrates." *

Allopathic "medical men," required two thousand years to "examine, sift, and form their deliberate and positive verdict" respecting the utter absurdity of the theoretical tenets of Hippocrates—the humoral pathology. If arithmetic be invoked, according to the custom of our opponents in regard to imponderable doses, it will probably be ascertained that eighteen or twenty additional centuries will be required to enable these

* *Sydenham's Processus Integri*, London, 1707, p. 53–4.

profound and "close reasoning" individuals to "examine, sift, and pass their deliberate and positive verdicts" upon the absurdity and destructiveness of the humoral treatment to which this pathology gave rise! Some of these deliberate gentlemen have firmly believed for two hundred years, that diseases consist in derangements of the vital properties of parts, and that the exciting causes of these derangements are for the most part dynamic, infinitesimal, and imponderable. In view of these doctrines, it would be natural to suppose that dynamic, infinitesimal and imponderable remedial agents would be selected to act on such vital properties, and to counteract such subtile exciting causes! But no, Allopathy deliberates slowly, and as the *humoral practice* of blood-letting, vomiting, purging, sweating, blistering, together with Dr. Sydenham's redoubtable "powders of bull's tail," &c., and the "volatile spirit and salt of vipers" are quite as important, and demand as close "examination and sifting" as the remarkable theory respecting the "four humors," above mentioned, a "deliberate and positive verdict" cannot reasonably be expected until about the year of grace, 4,000. Then, if the final conflagration shall not have converted this world into infinitesimal molecules, including the very material and substantial Dr. Hooker himself, a more appropriate dynamic system of treatment may be anticipated, such as should legitimately be deduced from a vital theory of diseases.

We have remarked that a few of our opponents, after abandoning the humoral pathology which had served them for two thousand years, became vitalists in theory. They now suppose that most diseases are produced by derangements of certain spiritual properties pertaining to the organism—derangements of the vital principle. Respecting the nature of this principle, and the manner in which derangements of it operate in causing disease, their ideas are as various as they are vague and unsatisfactory. It is a theory which admits of Dr. Hooker's "very extended, and very diversified combination" of explanations, and which serves most admirably for the indulgence of the wild and reckless spirit of *theorizing* which is so characteristic of Allopathy. By its aid, all things can be explained, all contradictory opinions can be reconciled, and all questions of a difficult or complicated nature can be readily solved. Thus, a dyspeptic desires his physician to inform him of the nature of his malady; and he receives the highly satisfactory reply that there is an "impaired condition of the vital powers of the stomach," and the inquisitive hypochondriac is informed that his "nervous system is laboring under a loss of vital energy"—that his headache and bad dreams proceed from "disorder of the upper sympathies," while the weakness and trembling of his limbs are dependent on "derangement of the lower sympathies."

We doubt whether any means could have been devised, so well calculated to cover over the ridiculous inconsistencies of Allopathy, as this arbitrary assumption of an immaterial and intangible principle. It admits of a "very extended and very diversified combination" of significations, from nothing at all up to the infinite variety of opinions entertained by this portion of the Old School. But it must be admitted that this is a very *convenient* theory, especially when patients are too inquisitive in regard to the nature of their ailments.

With respect to the other theoretical tenets pertaining to Allopathy, they are quite too numerous and too indefinite to render an enumeration of them at all interesting or feasible. To do this subject justice, it would be necessary to record the individual opinions of every gentleman of the school, as no two of them entertain precisely the same views respecting the intimate nature and treatment of disease. We see this truth verified in the wranglings and dissensions which are constantly occurring in their colleges, societies, conventions, and private consultations. Much care is generally taken to keep their differences of opinion from the public, in order that the system may not become universally distrusted; but now and then the "cloven foot" appears, as in the case of Dr. Rodgers, and the disgusting empiricism of Allopathy is fully displayed.

That the public may be furnished with a few reliable data on which to found an opinion respecting the competency of our opponents as a class to act as arbiters concerning the truth or falsity of medical doctrines, we subjoin a few of the theories which have met their approbation since the abandonment of the humoral pathology. The works from which we quote were standard allopathic treatises on theory and practice at the different periods alluded to, viz.: 1587, 1679, 1703, 1707, 1714, 1797, 1800, 1852.

1. Allopathy of 1587. "*Angina* is the Latin word.

In English it is named *Quincy*, the which is an imposthume in the throte, the which doth let a man to swallow either meat or drink.

" *The cause of this infirmitie.*

"This infirmitie doth come of reume ascending from the head to the throte. And it may come of vaporous humours, discending from the stomache to the throte.

"*A remedie.*

"Three things is requisite to help these infirmities: The *first* is letting of blood in a vayne named Cephalica. The *second* is to purge the head with the pilles of Cochée. And the *third* is to use gargarices, and to take a little piece of porke or bacon, or else a little piece of a sponge, and enoint it in oyle olive, and tie about any of these things a strong thred, and let the patient swallow in this matter and by and by pull it out againe, and be sure of the thred that he that shall do this feate, in holding fast the thred, doe pull it out againe quicklie." (*The Breviary of Health, &c., compyled by Andrew Boord, Doctor of Physicke: an English-man. Imprinted at London, by Thomas East.* 1587.)

In writing of *pleurisy* the same author remarks: "In English it is named a pleuresy, which is an imposthume in the ceneritie of the bones, but there be two kinds, the one is inward, and the other is in the gristles of the bones, and the other is in the lacertes in the brest, and Isaac saith that it is an hot imposthume that is ingendered in the midriffe named diaphragme."

"*The cause of this infirmitie.*

"This infirmitie doth come of a fumish blood, and of an hastie heart, which doth perturbate either the joynts, or else the heart and stomache with the brest.

"*A remedie.*

"First, if the part be constipated, take easy purgatives, as cassia fistula, and I have knowne old ancient doctors in this matter use phlebothomie, the which I did never use in this matter, considering the periculisnes of it."

The following were the views of Andrew Boord, M.D., respecting mania: "In English it is named he or they the which be mad and possessed of the devill or devills, and their propertie is to hurte and kill themselves, or else to hurte and kill any other thinge, therefore let every man beware of them and keepe them in a sure custody."

For the cure of this malady Dr. Boord advises that patients be sent to Rome; "for within the precinct of St. Peter's church without St. Peter's chappel, standeth a pillar of white marble grated round about with iron, to the which our Lord Jesus Christ did lye in himselfe at his delivering unto Pilot, as the Romans doth say, to the which pillar all those that be possessed of the devill, out of divers countries and nations, be brought thether, and as they say of Rome, such persons be made there whole. Among all other a woman of Germany, which is 400 miles and odde from Rome, was brought to the pillar, I there being present, with great strength and violently this woman was put into that pillar within the iron grate, and after her did go in a priest, and did examine the woman under this manner, in the Italian tongue. Thou devill or devills, I doe abjure thee by the potentiall power of the Father, and of the Sonne our Lord Jesus Christ, and by the virtue of the Holy Ghost, that thou doe show to me for what cause that thou doest possess this woman: what words was answered, I will not write, for men will not believe it, but wolde say it were a foule and greate lye, but I did hear that I was afrayd to tarry any longer, lest that the devills should have come out of her and to have entered into me, remembering what is specified in the chapter of St. Matthew, when that Jesus Christ had made two men whole, the which was possessed of a legion of devills." (p. 5.)

The writer enters into a learned discussion as to whether the great efficacy of the cure was attributable to the pillar or to the holy words of the priest; and after "examining and sifting" the evidences in the case he forms "a most deliberate and positive verdict" in favor of the latter.

Allopathy of 1679.* According to the "English Hippocrates," *Sydenham*, "*Jaundice* is caused by the diminution, loss, or decay of the animal salt in man's body," and the following remedies are advised as especially valuable: "Volatile salts of earth worms,

*Praxis Medica, of Sydenham, London, 1679, p. 451-2-4-6.

hog's lice, serpents, and toads: or skins of hens' gizzards, and of their feet, skins of geese feet, of each in powder, a drachm: volatile salts of urine, of earth worms, and of millepedes, of each a scruple: saffron in powder, 15 grains; mix them for four doses, to be given in extract of juniper berries, every morning fasting: or the ashes of sparrows' feathers, brain of partriges, lice, hog's lice, galls of hogs, and powders of viper's flesh, is approved by *Helmont* as a most excellent thing. *Paracelsus* especially commends "the juice extracted from the excrements of animals, mixed with white wine, and given as a drink." "*Willis* highly commends lice (though a nasty medicine) to be given alive, nine at a time, because they are full of *volatile animal salt.*" "*Silvius* commends the volatile spirit of urine, as a specific in jaundice."

These distinguished allopathists do not by any means omit emetics and cathartics in their treatment of jaundice, but they prescribe these "evacuators" in the first instance, in order to prepare the system for the reception of the above enumerated "specifics which restore and fix the animal salt."

Respecting the causes and pathology of jaundice, the respectable father of modern Allopathy, Sydenham, "dissents from all authors, both ancient and modern, who have written before him." He particularly condemns the "Galenic pathology, which ascribes its cause to choler."

Allopathy of 1703-7-14. "Palsy proceeds from the obstruction of the passages, and the impotency of the animal spirits, as they are either narcotically affected, or being small in quantity, do not exert themselves with vigor enough."

The chief remedies advised are, "mercurial purgatives, powder of viper's flesh and viper's bones, volatile salts of earth worms, man's hair, and of *dried human flesh*, (which is inferior to no other medicament)." (Dr. Sydenham's *Processus Integri*, p. 177.)

In the same work we find the following prescription for epilepsy: "Native cinnabar, man's skull filed, or philosophically calcined, elk's hoof, of each a drachm, powder of the heart and lungs of a mole, a drachm and a half, bezoarticum lunæ, crab's eyes levigated, of each a drachm, saffron a scruple, ambergrise, volatile laudanum, of each 5 grains; mix them—dose from a scruple to two scruples, according to age, in water of lilly convally flowers, and syrup of citron peels. Earth worms dried and powdered, and given to half a scruple, have been experimented effectual; so also the *ashes of a mole* given in like dose." (Ibid, p. 86.)

The following powders are highly praised as a remedy for bleeding at the nose, and hæmorrhages of different kinds: "Take of powder of man's blood, and of man's liver, dry'd, of each an ounce; powder of dry'd earth worms, and of catechu, of each half an ounce; ashes of an old hat, or so roasted that it may be rubbed to powder, hog's excrements, dry'd and powdered, of each one drachm; mix and divide into five powders for use." (Ibid, p. 255.)

From a standard allopathic work on the practice of medicine, we extract the following recipes: "Powder of wood lice prepared ℈iv, white poppy seed ℈i, powder of vipers ℈ii, mix—this is a powerful lythontriptic medicine, and ought to be had in estimation of all troubled with that disease; give the foresaid quantity at once in broth." (*Collectanea Medica*, London, 1703, p. 86.)

In the same work we find the following external application for quinsey: "One swallow's nest, album græcum, ℥jss, roots of althea, and of white lillies, of each one oz., figs and dates, of each three, boil them in water, and then add oyl of violets, three drachms, chamomile flowers, meal of Fenugreek-seed, linseed, wheat, of each six drachms, cat's brains, four drachms, powder of an owl burnt, of swallow's burnt, of each two drachms, one yolk of an egg, saffron, one scruple,—make a cataplasm. This cures a desperate quinsey." (p. 104.)

For colic, the writer recommends laudanum, and "drachm doses of powder of wolf's gut in wine," as a sovereign remedy.

In a standard French work on surgery, written in 1714, "by M. Le Clerc, physician and surgeon to the French King," we find the following prescriptions for cancer, which are declared specific: "A decoction of vipers, crab's eyes, adders and toads, may serve to bathe them, and some of it may be taken inwardly." The powders of mcles, toads, frogs, and crabs calcin'd, cleanse the ulcers perfectly well." (p. 166.)

Dr. Le Clerc speaks highly of calomel, and "viper's grease in doses of half a drachm," in syphilis.

During the early part of the 18th century, the

metaphysical views of Stahl were "examined and sifted" by the profession, and received their "deliberate and positive verdict" of approval. This sect was recognized under the name of *Animists* or *Spiritualists*. Taking into consideration the fact that solids and fluids when connected with the living body, are not subject to putrefaction, dissolution, and other ordinary laws of matter as when disconnected with it, Stahl superadded a spiritual principle which he termed *anima*, which was supposed to act in "opposition to the physical powers of matter, and to which the body owes all those properties that are strictly denominated vital. He supposes this principle to possess peculiar qualities, distinct from those which belong to matter; and he especially endowed it with a species of intelligence, or even consciousness, by which it acts the part of a rational agent, and is the general director of all the corporeal operations."

Among the distinguished physicians of the eighteenth century, who took a prominent part in sealing the "deliberate and positive verdict" in favor of the Stahlian hypothesis, were Sauvages, Whytt, Nicholls, Gaubius, Alberti, and Junker.

During the last half of the eighteenth century, another hypothesis was "examined and sifted" by this "close reasoning" profession, and a "deliberate and positive verdict" was rendered in favor of the "vital theory." "They have professed to ascertain the laws of the animal economy by actual observation, and by this means to discover what are the appropriate powers or qualities of the living body, and in what respect these powers or qualities differ from those of inanimate or unorganized matter."

It is true that during this century there were a few sensible men, who, reasoning from the medical absurdities of the past, repudiated all hypotheses, and declared themselves *eclectics*. These men evidently entertained a profound contempt for the whole system of Allopathy, and wisely determined to keep aloof from all hypotheses, and trust to Providence in the treatment of disease, until a rational system of medicine should be discovered. These early eclectics were apparently honest. They appreciated the fallacies of every medical doctrine which had been broached, and prepared to arm their book of knowledge and remain "non-committal," until something reasonable and demonstrable should be proposed, rather than to accept any of the visionary tenets which were then in vogue.

As the nineteenth century dawned upon the world, the science of medicine presented a singular spectacle. Instead of a rational and consistent theory of disease, and a uniform system of cure founded upon well-ascertained facts, medical men were divided into animists, vitalists, solidists, chemists, eclectics, Brunonians, Cullenists, mechanicians, expectants, etc. But notwithstanding these numerous and contradictory theoretical doctrines, no new practical tenets were deduced, but the humoral treatment of blood-letting, purging, vomiting, sweating, stimulating, blistering, &c., were still prescribed, although in a most vague and contradictory manner. For the same malady one sect advised bleeding and purging;

another sect denounced this treatment as fatal, and commended stimulants; another class prescribed chemical alteratives; another emetics and diaphoretics; another opiates and gum-water, and so on *ad infinitum.*

Thus has Allopathy continued up to the present moment—a gigantic system of *theorizing* from absurd and imaginary data. During the two thousand years in which the allopathic "verdict" was fixed in favor of the humoral pathology, this reckless spirit of theorizing was expended in experimenting upon poor humanity with almost every conceivable and *outre* substance, from blood-letting and physic, down to toads, adders, bull's tail, man's scull, and viper's grease. But from the middle of the seventeenth century to the present time, the "most extended and diversified combination of systems—modes—and kinds of practice," have been pursued by our opponents that can possibly be conceived of, so that human life has been made the play-thing of various sects of legalized empyrics. Ever ready to practically test their absurd hypotheses, and their guess-work prescriptions upon others, it is a notorious fact that they have very rarely had the courage or we should rather say desperation, to try the same experiments upon *themselves or their families.*

Assuming to herself vast knowledge and respectability—denying the ability of the public to judge respecting medical matters—boasting of her great antiquity, and of her accumulated facts of two thousand years, modern Allopathy has entrenched herself behind her enormous self-conceit, surrounded by envy, hate, malice, and vindictive slander, as body guards. She has indeed grown hoary and withered—spotted all over with the errors and fallacies of many centuries; but her past history and her past deeds do not elicit any marks of respect or gratitude from the world, or give rise to any agreeable reminiscences; but innumerable phantoms, pale, haggard, and sepulchral, ever hover around her, fit emblems of her past and present existence. Under the accumulated weight of so many mistakes and inconsistencies, she totters and trembles, and her former boldness is gone; but she still survives, the shameless wreck of numerous exploded systems of absurdities .She still survives —her destructive instincts still remain, and she still glares around in search of more victims, but modern science is rapidly extracting her fangs and impairing her pernicious influence.

In regard to the inuendoes, and "the very extended, and very diversified combination" of epithets, denunciations, and false accusations so freely indulged in by her unamiable satellites towards homœopathic physicians and their numerous and intelligent patrons, we might retort by resorting to counter denunciations and counter accusations, but such a course would degrade us to a level with our allopathic traducers, from which may the Lord ever deliver us. The veriest vagabond at the Five Points can call as hard names, and make as false assertions, as even the author of the "Evidences" himself, and we have no doubt that both would exercise about an eqnal amount of influence upon the public mind. Homœopathists prefer that intelligent laymen, who are the parties chiefly interested in the matter, should decide respecting the comparative merits of the two classes of practitioners, confident that the verdict will not be in favor of those who boast most of their own qualifications, or are most lavish in the use of vulgar abuse.

We ask, then, if it is proper that medical doctrines should be submitted to the advocates of Allopathy for a "verdict"? Is it reasonable to suppose that Hahnemann and his followers would submit their theory of cure to the tender mercies of their opponents, after a single glance at the past history of medical doctrines? The Hahnemannian principle strikes at the foundation of the whole allopathic fabric, and the points at issue involve the very *existence* of one or the other method. There can be no mixing of practices, no "very extended and very diversified combinations" of principles, and no compromise of any description between the two schools, for their doctrines are directly opposite to each other, so that one side must of necessity be all wrong. For this reason we should as soon think of placing the Christian religion before Satan for approval, as of submitting the truths of Homœopathy to the judgment of an Old School tribunal. These self-constituted judges may, for aught we know, be competent to deliberate upon *their own* doctrinal points, and form "positive verdicts" as to whether "maniack persons be possessed of devills," and whether the best treatment consists in putting them into the "white marble pillar of St. Peter's church at Rome," in order that the jurist may quiz the devils so closely as to induce them to take "French leave" of "he or she that be possessed;" or they may constitute a very appropriate medical jury to decide respecting the merits of the "volatile spirits and volatile salt of vipers, man's blood, urine," &c., and the "very extended and very diversified combination" of powders peculiar to Allopathy, like those of "bull's tail, dried toads, adders, wolf's gut, crab's eyes, old hat, earth worms, man's skull, hog lice, wood lice, human flesh, human liver," etc., etc., but we most emphatically deny their competency, both intellectually and morally, to render a just opinion respecting the merits of Homœopathy. The followers of Hahnemann will continue, therefore, to decline all these very kind offices of their vindictive opponents, and trust, as usual, to the spontaneous verdicts which are daily being rendered by a discriminating public.

Dr. Hooker asserts that only a few of the eminent men of his school have embraced Homœopathy, and that this is presumptive evidence of its unsoundness. This mode of combatting truth is not new, as any one may be convinced by looking back upon all past discoveries of any real value. When Christ and his humble disciples proclaimed to the world the glorious truths of the Christian religion, nearly all of the learned and powerful men of that period, especially the priests and other members of the "clerical profession," denounced our Saviour as an impostor, and his doctrines as fallacies. After he had continued his mission through a long series of years, and multitudes of the people had been convinced of the truth of what he taught, the argument of this "profession" then was, "behold our rabbis, our priests, our wise men, our men in authority,—do not they adhere to their ancient gods, their idols, and their accumulated facts of centuries?" "Have they not passed their verdict against the religion of Christ in the most deliberate manner? and can such an holy, learned and ancient profession be wrong?" These allopathic rabbis and their abettors carried out their verdict in a practical manner by nailing our Saviour to the cross; but all of their persecutions and false accusations did not for an instant arrest the diffusion of the Gospel among the people.

The same rabbinical motives now actuate the professors of Allopathy in their opposition to Homœopathy. The most eminent of them are in receipt of large incomes from extensive practices, from professorships in medical colleges, from positions in hospitals, and from other lucrative offices, and they cannot *afford* to acknowledge the truth of Homœopathy, for by so doing they would be cast out of the allopathic synagogue, with a prospect of loss of business, and starvation staring them in the face. These distinguished Old School gentlemen are altogether human and prudential—they know their own interests too well to forsake their ancient idols—they prefer to remain sleek and comfortable, and to be drawn about the streets by pairs of good-blooded and comfortable horses, rather than to run the risk of being nailed to an allopathic cross. And then these well-conditioned gentlemen are quite aware of the time and labor it would require to learn the homœopathic doctrines so as to be able to practice them properly, and this again deters them from even an investigation of the subject. So likewise, pride of opinion, long standing and deep-rooted prejudices, and reverence for ancient names and ancient doctrines stand in the way, as formidable barriers against all novel ideas and all original thought. And again it requires a large amount of moral courage to meet the sneers, the ribald imputations, and the reckless slanders of the baser members of the profession, who make it a point to assail every one who dares dissent from the abominations of the Old School. Timid and sensitive men, therefore, not unfrequently persist in upholding doctrines which they know to be erroneous, through dread of the attacks of these medical Jesuits.

At page 140, Dr. Hooker observes: "If we compare the therapeutics of the present day with that which prevailed fifty or a hundred years ago, medication is vastly more cautious and discriminating than it was then, and the movements of nature, in the cure of disease, are much more narrowly observed. And, at this time, there are multitudes of minds in the profession on the right track in their inquiries; and we have reason to anticipate that great advances will now be rapidly made in the practical part of our science." The evidences of this are daily witnessed in the sly adoption of homœopathic remedies into allopathic practice. Even so late as ten years ago, the use of *aconite*, in bilious remittent, and other fevers, of *belladonna* in scarlatina, of *camphor* in cholera, of *arnica* in mechanical injuries, and of *rhus* in erysipelas, would have been deemed rank heresy by our opponents; but if we examine the allopathic "therapeutics of the present day," we shall see that all of these homœopathic specifics are now in common use, and that they are highly commended in some of their journals, as new and important allopathic discoveries!

It is difficult to believe that a learned profession can descend to such meanness as to *steal*, in cool blood, the discoveries of another, and seek to appropriate them to its own credit, while at the same time it has the insolence to denounce their author as a "quack," a "dreamer in science," etc.

There is no doubt that the celebrated Liston was "on the right track in his enquiries," for several years previous to his death, as his frequent employment of belladonna and rhus in erysipelas, and a variety of other homœopathic medicines in different diseases, amply prove. There is no question but that Dr. Lyon, physician to St. Bartholomew's hospital, of London, is "on the right track," if we may judge from his excellent paper in the "Lancet," of the —— ——, on the value of belladonna as a specific in scarlet fever. There is no doubt but that all of those Old School gentlemen "are on the right track," who at the present time so often employ aconite in fevers, coffea, nux vomica, belladonna, and aconite, in neuralgic affections, ipecac. in asthma and nausea and vomiting, phosphorus in pneumonia, etc. For their own sakes, and for the welfare of their patients, we sincerely congratulate these enquirers of the profession upon this tendency they now evince, of placing themselves upon the "right track" in therapeutics. A little more moral courage, a little more independence of thought, and a little more industry, gentlemen eclectics, and you may yet get entirely into the "right track," and become useful members of the homœopathic profession.

In the last pages of his essay, Dr. Hooker alludes to Homœopathy as a system of "medical radicalism," and to her advocates, as "radicals in medicine," and like a starving mendicant, implores "the intelligent and influential in the community" not to encourage this radicalism, but to "throw around his profession all those safeguards which are needed to secure its advancement." In lieu of any arguments to sustain his assertion, or of any reasons why his modest request should be granted, he resorts to the same wise and profound philosophy which pervades his entire attack, in the form of the most "extended and diversified combination" of epithets, that we have ever seen strung together.

His style of logic is something like this: "Homœopathy is a system of medical radicalism," and *therefore* "medical delusion," "fallacy," "quackery," "imposture," "absurdity," "ephemeral folly," "patent nostrums," "fantasies,' "fanatical," "loose reasoners," etc., etc. The advocates of Homœopathy possess the very spirit of radicalism," *therefore*, "quack," impostor," "ignoramus," "dreamers," "scientific fools," "loose analyzers," "cheats," "uneducated," "irresponsible," etc., etc.

It is certainly a *novel* if not a *conclusive* mode of attacking a rival system, to make an arbitrary assertion, and then to ransack Webster's dictionary for abusive words with which to sustain it. This may be a very shrewd "Yankee trick" in medical dialectics, but ill not suit the intellectual palates of the "intelligent and influential in the community," any better than the equally ingenious "trick" of palming off wooden nutmegs and wooden hams, as genuine articles, would agree with their gustatory faculties.

But let us briefly examine this "medical radicalism" of which Dr. Hooker speaks, and endeavor to ascertain what class of physicians are really entitled to the appellation of "medical radicals."

The term radicalism is usually applied to any extreme theory, which recognizes no fixed laws, and which appropriates to itself hypotheses from all sources, without proofs to substantiate their validity, and without any regard to logical induction. A system, therefore, which is constantly changing its ground—which advocates one thing to-day and another thing to-morrow—which professes theoretical ideas of the most ultra, diverse and contradictory character, while in practice it recognizes a mode of treatment founded upon an universally conceded absurdity, may with great justice be termed a *radical* system.

Let us now make an application of Dr. Hooker's definition of Allopathy, and see whether or not the "coat fits." "But what is Allopathy? Is it one thing—one mode—one system? By no means. This term is applied to all kinds of practice pursued by all regular physicians. It is a very extended, and very diversified combination. It includes much that is good, and much that is bad. And the practitioners of this Allopathy are, some of them, bad practitioners." (p. 100.)

Here is "radicalism in medicine" with a vengeance. It has not even the saving virtue of being entitled to the rank of a specious and plausible radicalism; for it has no limits, it recognizes no bounds, but appropriates "all modes—all systems—all things, and all kinds of practice," from the heroic and humoral remedies of the fathers of ancient Allopathy, Hippocrates and Galen, down to the "viper's grease" and "powders of old hat," of the fathers of modern Allopathy, Helmont and Sydenham.

It is conceded on all hands that Allopathy has no fixed and permanent basis, either in theory or practice, and therefore, that each medical man must exercise his own private judgment respecting the nature and treatment of each case to which he may be called. The very largest liberty is allowed him in forming his opinion, and therefore, he explores the whole boundless universe of Allopathy, from the foundation of medicine to the present time, selecting here an idea and there an idea, as best suits his particular fancy, and then brings these scattered and arbitrary notions to bear in treating the sick. To-day one theory and one kind of practice prevail: to-morrow an ingenious theorizer brings forward a new set of views, and a new mode of practice, and the doctrines of yesterday are overthrown. Changes, innovations, and radicalism, of the most ultra description have been eminently characteristic of Allopathy, from the abandonment of the Hippocratic and Galenic pathology, to the present moment. The human stomach has been looked upon and used by this school, as an experimental laboratory wherein her advocates might practically test their numerous and contradictory hypotheses. In carrying out such experiments, she has always had the shrewdness to operate upon the *sick* only, so that all unfortunate results like ruined constitutions, and deaths, caused by enormous quantities of drugs, could be placed to the account of natural disease. In this way the direful effects of this medical radicalism have, to a certain extent, been kept from the public. Let the impartial reader look into those families of his acquaintance which have been subjected to this radical system of drugging for a considerable period, and see how few he can find upon whom the blighting marks of Allopathy are not permanently impressed. Let him consider the pale and sickly features, the fetid brea hs, the black and carious teeth, the trembling, stiff and painful limbs, the nervousness, and the morbid sensitiveness of the victims of mercury: or the waxen faces, the bloated forms, and indurated livers of those who have been poisoned with quinine: or the unfortunate dyspeptics and hypochondriacs whose lives have been made wretched by cathartics: or the impaired and sickly constitutions of those who have been habitually bled and narcotized with opiates: or the organic disorders of the heart and lungs, which have been produced by tartar emetic and copaibæ: or any of the numerous medicinal diseases under which so many over-drugged mortals are suffering, and then decide whether this system is not one which is eminently entitled to the appellation of "medical radicalism," and whether its practitioners are not "radicals of the most dangerous character."

The political radical, who believes in the doctrine, "*propriété c'est le vol*," and who contends for a division of property, a plurality of wives, and for the appropriation to his own purposes of everything which happens to suit his fancy or convenience, is certainly a dangerous member of community, and his principles, were they generally carried out, would undermine the foundations of society, and lead directly to social anarchy and confusion. He believes himself entitled to the largest kind of liberty, both in theory and practice, and explores the entire records of history for precedents to sustain his views, from the polygamous Solomon of old, to the social and variety-loving Mormon of the present day. Dr. Hooker's definition of modern Allopathy applies admirably to his contemporary political system which has been announced by Proudhom and Joseph Smith. Like its prototype, it is not "one thing—one mode—one system: by no means. This term (socialism) is applied to all kinds of practice pursued by all regular physicians (socialists). It is a very extended and a very diversified combination. It includes much that is good, and much that is bad. And the practitioners of this Allopathy (socialism) are, some of them, bad practitioners."

But if the *political* radical, in practically testing his eclectic and empirical views, endangers the integrity and purity of the social fabric, what shall be said of the *medical* radical who practically experiments, with his equally empirical processes upon the diseased human fabric? The socialist radical contaminates and impairs the principles of men; the medical radical poisons their bodies. The course of the one leads to immorality and vice, that of the other to permanent illness, suffering, and premature death.

CHAPTER VII.

CONCLUDING OBSERVATIONS.

From the foregoing observations, the profession and the community will remark that the Hippocratic school of the present day is actuated by the same intolerant spirit which has always characterized it since the days of Hippocrates and Galen. The very distinction of the subject of medicine—the uncertainty and mystery pertaining to the intimate nature of disease, and the *modus operandi* of remedial agents—the proneness of mankind to measure all things by previous knowledge—the influence of long established dogmas, and the deeply-rooted prejudices they have engendered—the momentous interests at stake in connection with the practice of the art, have each tended to encompass the subject with difficulties, and thus enable the intolerant, the bigoted, the selfish, and the designing of the profession to exercise an undue influence over the general mind. Whenever an original idea has been advanced which has happened to clash with any of the "accumulated facts of ages," the medical rabbis who preside over the shrine of ancient Allopathy, have ever been on the alert, and by denunciations, persecution, and various forms of oppression, have generally succeeded in crushing all fresh investigation at the onset.

From these circumstances the reader may understand why medicine has made so little progress in comparison with other sciences, until the time of Hahnemann. While anatomy has unfolded the intricate structures of the human organism, and physiology has explained the functions of its different parts—while chemistry has developed, from the hidden treasures of the animal, vegetable, and mineral kingdoms, substances both ponderable and imponderable, possessed of properties of the most potent efficiency—while botany, mineralogy, the microscope, and a philosophical mode of induction, have all been made available, within the past century, for purposes of scientific improvements in every branch of human knowledge, the healing art has slumbered on in its prolonged sleep of centuries, disturbed only by the occasional nightmare of an original idea which has by chance flitted before it. Instead of examining, and of endeavoring to appreciate the delicate and subtile phenomena of the human body in health and in disease, and the almost unlimited powers of imponderable agents in modifying the condition of all its parts, at all times, and under all circumstances, Allopathy has chosen to retain the material and gross ideas of antiquity as her guides in the treatment of disease. Precisely the same remedial means are employed now, empirically and at random, it is true, which were used by the heathen allopathists twenty-two hundred years ago, when alchemy, sorcery and astrology held the rank which chemistry, anatomy and physiology now hold. The crude notions of these early physicians are excusable, on the ground of their utter ignorance respecting the phenomena of life, and of the vast powers of imponderable agents in their chemical, morbific, and remedial operations upon material structures; but the obstinacy and wilful blindness of their modern brethren, with regard to these important subjects, is not only inexcusable, but deserving of the severest censure.

No class of men, however strong their position may have become from circumstances which have long been in operation, has the right to trifle with human life and human happiness, by endeavoring to repress investigations which threaten to clash with their antiquated prejudices, or to overthrow their preconceived dogmas. No body of men has the right, or will be permitted, at this enlightened period, to act as judges and dictators of the opinions of others, or to exercise any permanent influence against an opponent by private calumnies, collegiate persecutions, or legislative enactments. The days of the inquisition have long since fled, and no medical Loyola can now plot and conspire against the promulgation of knowledge and truth. The ideas of Homœopathy may still be assailed by the impotent denunciations and the senseless ridicule of the ignorant and conceited of the Old School, as heretofore, but Homœopathy will continue to advance until the crumbling fabric of Allopathy shall be prostrate, and the only rational system of medicine established in its place.

From much observation during a practice of fifteen years, first as an allopathist and then as a homœopathist, we are quite satisfied that the practitioners of the Old School, as a body, are entirely ignorant of the doctrines of Homœopathy. This is daily illustrated in their constant assertions that the remedies of the two schools are the same, and that the only difference consists in the fact that the allopath uses these drugs in a crude state, while the homœopath uses them in an infinitesimal form. In their allusions to the subject, they almost invariably leave out of the question the real points at issue between the two systems, and confine themselves to the incidental point of doses. How often do we hear the remark by the Old School physician that this or that medicine is allopathic, without any reference to the disease or symptoms for which it is employed; thus leaving the impression that both schools administer the same remedies in the same diseases! How studiously do they conceal the fact that one class of practitioners doctor the stomach, intestines, and skin, for nearly all diseases, while the other class direct their remedial applications to diseased parts only. With how much assumed importance and gusto do the smaller men of the profession presume to sit in judgment on Hahnemann, and with sardonic grimaces discharge their intellectual popguns at infinitesimal doses, while the towering citadel of *similia similibus curantur* receives not a single paper wad. Occasionally, however, a man of extraordinary courage, like Dr. Hooker, dares to notice our law of cure. But even in these instances we regret to perceive that the spirit of the homœopathic principle is entirely misunderstood and misrepresented. These writers have evidently given only a superficial glance at the therapeutical law of Hahnemann, without any desire to understand and appreciate its importance, but for the express purpose of opposing and ridiculing it. It is for this reason that all of their attacks upon the subject have proved futile, and, for the most part, unworthy of consideration.

It is only within the past year or two that Homœopathy has been considered worthy of any extended notice. For more than twenty years its opponents have constantly asserted that it was losing ground everywhere, and that it would speedily be forgotten. It is even implied by our cyphering friend, Dr. Hooker, that Hahnemannism is going down both in this country and in Europe, and now, since the profession, through him, "has passed its verdict against it," that it will soon be blotted out of existence. If collegiate oppressions, printed and oral calumnies, and such influences as the most vindictive hatred of the old school profession can suggest, can retard its progress and extinguish its utility, these predictions may be verified; but as Hahnemann and his disciples have not committed the guardianship of their system to their bitter enemies, but to an intelligent and discriminating public, we entertain no misgivings respecting its ultimate destiny.

It is scarcely twenty-five years since the homœopathic mode of practice was introduced into America. Then, a single physician in New York was its only representative; but, to quote from Dr. Curtis's Inaugural Address, of January 14, 1852:

"Between this single voice then raised in its favor, and the present response, what a contrast! Fifteen hundred physicians of our land now own its worth and dispense its resources. It is the just panegyric of our school that these are not adventurers, who have overleaped the walls of privilege and the qualifications of teaching, but, with the rarest exceptions, men of accredited ability in the received systems of medicine, who, from a catholic regard for truth, have embraced Homœopathy, and brought their badges of professional merit as a graceful offering to its superiority; their verdict for it is the voluntary suffrage of adepts. And who are the non-professional advocates of the new method? They are a large and brilliant clientage, who have brought Homœopathy to the touchstone of experience, and whose culture, judgment and liberality are its pride and hope."

And what shall be said of the present condition of Homœopathy in Europe? Within the last year the University of Edinburgh has established a medical inquisition, for the purpose of excluding from its privileges all those students who may dare to think or form their own opinions upon medical subjects. The allopathic professors of this institution have assumed to themselves the attributes of medical infallibility, and now essay to violate the intelligences of their pupils by forcing upon them, *nolens volens*, their own contradictory hypotheses, to the absolute exclusion of every idea which smacks of Hahnemannism. Other medical schools are also on the *qui vive*, and are only deterred by public opinion from issuing their bulls of excommunication against all who presume to differ from them in opinion. Medical journals which, a few years since, scarcely deemed the New School worthy of a passing inuendo, now teem with sophistries and calumnies against it of the most Jesuitical and vindictive character.

In London two respectable homœopathic hospitals have been established within the past year under the patronage and management of such men as the Duke of Beaufort, the Archbishop of Dublin, Lord Robert Grosvenor, and the Marquis of Anglesey. Other hospitals have also been founded in several of the larger towns of England under the auspices of the most noble and intelligent of the land. Numerous dispensaries likewise distribute their blessings in every quarter, and by their successes in practice, contribute much towards the extension of the system.

In France, one of the most learned and intelligent medical men of Paris, Dr. Tessier, physician to the *Hôpital Sainte Marguerite*, (one of the hospitals connected with the *Hôtel Dieu*, and containing one hundred beds,) after a careful preliminary study of the writings of Hahnemann, and a rigid practical investigation respecting their truth at the bedside of the sick, for a period of more than two years, has publicly announced the vast superiority of this mode of practice over the antiphlogistic measures of the Old School. When it is known that the principal diseases treated by Dr. Tessier were pneumonia (lung fever) and cholera, the importance of the result will be better appreciated.

With respect to the gentleman himself, who has thus been converted to Homœopathy, the simple fact of his appointment to the post of physician to a hospital like that of *Sainte Marguerite*, proves the estimation put upon his talents while an allopathic practitioner, but now, as he has changed his opinions upon medical topics, he will of course be classed among the "deluded," "loose reasoning," "uneducated and irresponsible" followers of Hahnemann.

In Austria, Russia, and several other countries of continental Europe, well endowed homœopathic hospitals are in successful operation, and the practice is everywhere extending among the intelligent classes.

It is a fact eminently worthy of notice that the patrons of Homœopathy are among the most intellectual and well-educated of every nation.

Dr. Hooker has chosen to refer in terms of reproach to the clergy for the willingness they have evinced to accept the doctrines of the philosophical school in medicine, and he has expended besides abortive wit, no inconsiderable amount of contumelious invective against this class, which, to say nothing of the consideration in which it should be held, for its sacred functions, embraces a larger amount of learning, talent, and logical acumen, than any other in the world. We may confess that we are proud that the members of a profession so intelligent, learned, and conscientious, have so generally examined and approved the homœopathic theory, and adopted its practice; but would it not have been more appropriate for Dr. Hooker to have discussed the more material and important fact, that of the thoroughly educated, right-minded, and *successful practitioners* of the Old School, so large a number have been converted to the doctrines of Hahnemann? *This* is the exciting cause of the indignation, jealousy, and mortification of the allopathic practitioners, and for this they can offer no plausible reason, except the apparent and overwhelming truth of our system.

We have hastily and imperfectly, yet we trust satisfactorily answered the so-called "examinations" of Dr. Worthington Hooker; and we think we have shown him to be as deficient in common honesty and conscience as he is in a knowledge and fit judgment of the true principles of cure. With a worthier antagonist, and more time, we might have entered into a more elaborate, perhaps a more satisfactory investigation of those great principles in medicine, which are destined to have supreme acceptance and the most satisfactory influence among the intelligent classes of mankind.

For the present, we have done.

CPSIA information can be obtained at www.ICGtesting.com
Printed in the USA
LVOW101457210911

247272LV00002B/4/P

9 781425 511128